100 THINGS TO DO IN DULUTH BEFORE YOU DIE

Bent Paddle Brewing

100 THINGS TO DO IN DULUTH BEFORE YOU DIE

JAY GABLER

REEDY PRESS

Reedy Press
PO Box 5131
St. Louis, MO 63139, USA
reedypress.com

Library of Congress Control Number: 2024949287

ISBN: 9781681065502

Design by Jill Halpin

Cover photo courtesy of Zenith Adventure

Unless otherwise noted, all photos are courtesy of the author or believed to be in the public domain.

Printed in the United States of America
26 27 28 29 5 4 3 2

DEDICATION

Dedicated to the great friends I met in Duluth as a child, and to the equally great Duluth friends I've made since moving back.

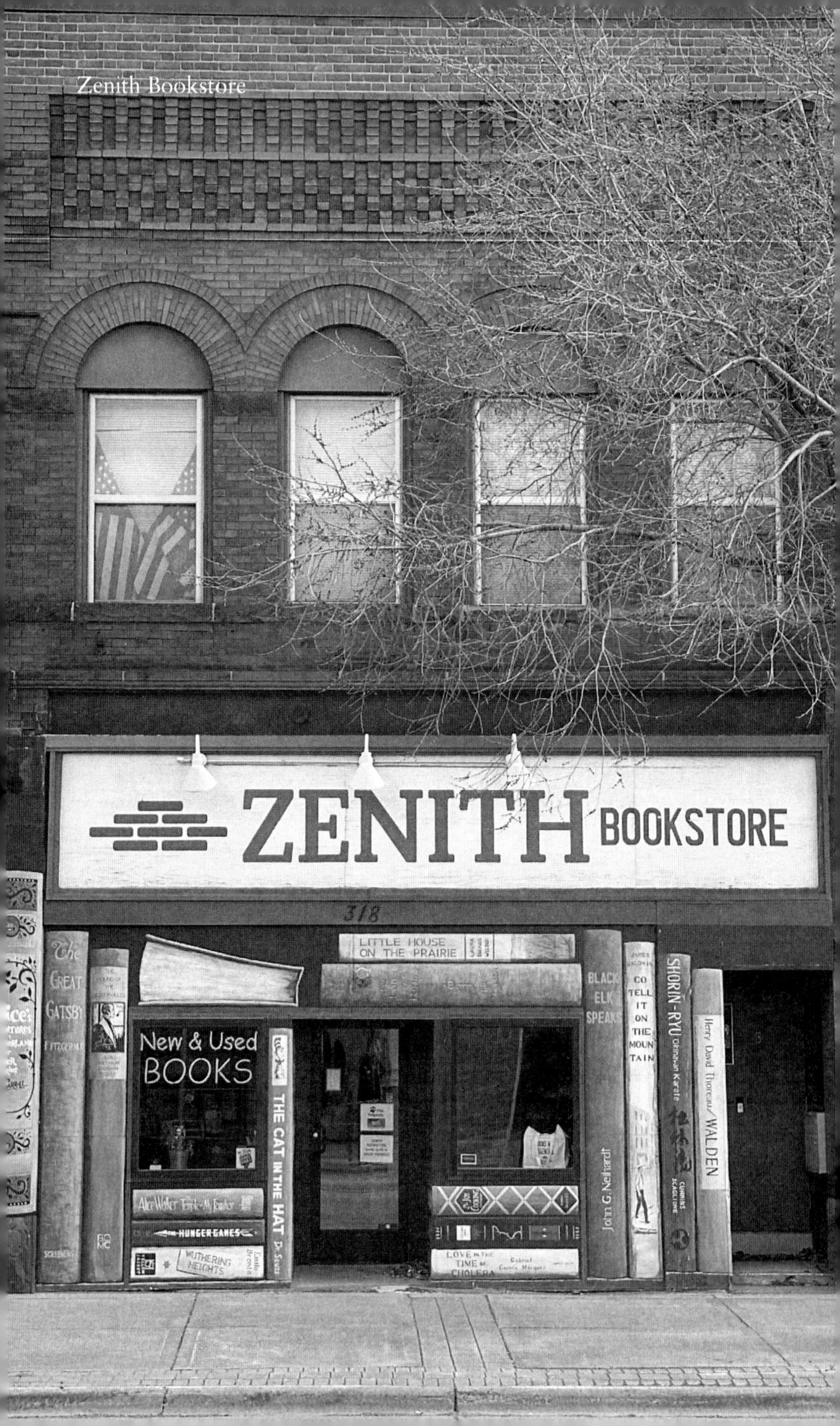

Zenith Bookstore

CONTENTS

Music and Entertainment

Sports and Recreation

ACKNOWLEDGMENTS

Thanks to Tony Dierckins for recommending me when he heard that Reedy Press was looking to commission this book. I also appreciate the support I've received from Amanda Doyle, Xavier Stevens, and the rest of the Reedy Press staff. Although this book was written independent of my work as arts and entertainment reporter at the *Duluth News Tribune*, it benefited from the local knowledge I've picked up in that job, and I owe a debt of gratitude to my colleagues at the paper for everything they've taught me. My Duluth friends—particularly Margie Nelson, Steve Wick, and Brittany Lind-Libby—have been incredibly kind in sharing their insiders' perspectives on this incomparable city and its many fascinating corners. Finally, love and appreciation to the two families I've lived with in Duluth: first my parents and siblings, and then my spouse and child. You've been the heart of all my Zenith City adventures.

Bob Dylan Pilgrimage

PREFACE

It's hard to wrap your mind around Duluth.

Duluth is a global port, but it sits smack in the middle of a continent. It's a boat city, but it's also a train town. It's known for being on Lake Superior, but technically speaking, much of the city's shoreline is actually along a harbor and a river. It's an industrial city, but it's also a tourist town. It's a hub of outdoor recreation, despite having famously punishing weather. It's on a hill, and yet it's prone to floods. Over the past half century, it's been radically transformed, and yet its population size has remained almost unchanged during that time.

The city's contradictions make for a diverse list of activities to tick off your Head of the Lakes bucket list. Some are easy to do (check out the ship-shaped library); some present more of a challenge (go surfing on Lake Superior). Choose your own adventure. However you do Duluth, you won't be bored.

Northern Waters Smokehaus

FOOD AND DRINK

1

TRY THE ONION RINGS
AT THE PICKWICK

The Pickwick kitchen is in the restaurant's basement. There's a room down there dedicated to the sole purpose of producing onion rings: onions freshly cut into slices thick enough to accommodate a substantial, crispy breading. They're a side dish that would threaten to outshine the main course if the restaurant didn't invest such care in the steaks and sandwiches that have made the Pickwick a reliable stop for generations of locals and travelers.

The restaurant is right next to Fitger's, and the proximity is no coincidence. The Pickwick traces its history to 1888, when it opened as a saloon within the brewery. It moved to its current building with a robustly Germanic vibe in 1914. Whether you're seeking cozy comfort safe from whipping winter winds or enjoying an interlude away from the summer sun, the Pickwick offers a taste of tradition and an inspiring view of Lake Superior.

508 E Superior St., 218-623-7425
pickwickduluth.com

TIP

From mid-November through New Year's, the Pickwick offers one of the country's best Tom and Jerry cocktails. A hot, creamy drink, the Tom and Jerry is a cherished regional tradition. If you want to continue your Tom and Jerry tour, try Thirsty Pagan Brewing and the Spirit Room, both across the harbor in Superior.

2

MARVEL AT A REVOLVING RESTAURANT:

HARBOR 360

In the mid-20th century, revolving restaurants were the last word in futuristic amenities for cities with a lot to see. Duluth certainly fit that bill, and in 1970 the city got a cylindrical Radisson with a turntable at the top. Today, the venue known locally as "the top of the Radisson" is among only a handful of active revolving restaurants still open for public dining in the US.

Officially known as Harbor 360, the restaurant doesn't overcomplicate its offerings in the culinary department. It's a hotel restaurant. The attraction is the view, as seen from tables that make a complete circuit in about an hour. You'll see the downtown skyline from a building in its midst; the hillside with its varied topography and even more varied architecture; and the harbor, from a perspective that will give you a new appreciation for the sheer scale of the massive freighters passing under the Aerial Lift Bridge.

505 W Superior St., 218-722-8439
harbor360duluth.com

3

EAT SMOKED FISH
AT NORTHERN WATERS SMOKEHAUS

Today Great Lakes commercial fishing is strictly limited to protect the ecosystem, but it's still possible to enjoy the whitefish and trout that have long been staples for Lake Superior locals. Smoking is a practical and delicious way to prepare the fish, and the proprietors of Northern Waters Smokehaus are masters of the art.

In a Canal Park space, expanded in 2023 to meet popular demand, Northern Waters offers a deli counter with local fish and other products to go—or you can order a sandwich featuring meats and fish from far and wide to enjoy right then and there. The Cajun Finn is by far the most popular choice, but follow your palate and you won't go wrong. (The menu also includes vegetarian options.)

Even if just passing through, experienced visitors order ahead online so their sandwiches will be ready to go for a quick bite on the road or during a pause by the lake.

394 Lake Ave. S, 218-724-7307
northernwaterssmokehaus.com

4

DISCOVER
"THE CRAFT BEER CAPITAL OF MINNESOTA"

In 2013, Don Ness, then mayor of Duluth, claimed that his city was "the Craft Beer Capital of Minnesota." Duluthians cheered the mayor's bold (if unofficial) declaration and have proudly claimed it ever since. The city's several breweries can draw on some of the country's best water, straight from Lake Superior. They also pride themselves on an elevated level of craft and care.

Bent Paddle is the city's best-known brewery, with a bustling Lincoln Park taproom that often hosts live music and events. Down the street, Ursa Minor boasts a family-friendly space and beers that pack a punch. Blacklist Brewing, specializing in Belgian brews downtown, offers axe throwing. Lake Superior Brewing, the city's oldest operating craft brewery, has food to savor.

For an almost overwhelming experience, hit the All Pints North Summer Brew Fest at Bayfront Festival Park. For craft beer lovers, it doesn't get any better than this.

To locate breweries and learn more about All Pints North:
mncraftbrew.org

5

EXPERIENCE NEW NORDIC CUISINE
AT NEW SCENIC CAFÉ

One of Duluth's most acclaimed restaurants is located just outside the city limits on what locals call "Scenic Highway 61." There's also a more recent, less scenic, Highway 61 running parallel inland.

There's a reason for the "new" in the name of New Scenic Café. Chef Scott Graden purchased the long-standing Scenic Café and reconceived it in 1999, giving Duluthians the then-unusual experience of a menu that emphasized culinary creativity and fresh ingredients. "I have to hire cooks from Outback or Olive Garden, and I have to untrain some of their beliefs and values," Graden told the *Star Tribune* in 2019.

The restaurant augured the rise of craft eateries across the Northland and reconnected the area with authentic Scandinavian approaches to staples like fish and vegetables. You'll be surprised by Graden's inventive takes with multicultural twists, incorporating French, Mexican, and Middle Eastern cuisine.

5461 North Shore Dr., 218-525-6274
newsceniccafe.com

SIP A COCKTAIL
MADE WITH LAKE SUPERIOR WATER—AND LOCALLY FORAGED BOTANICALS—AT VIKRE DISTILLERY

Duluth has several craft breweries and two craft cideries, but fewer craft distilleries. Fortunately, the city's best-known distillery is world class.

Vikre Distillery, owned by married couple Emily and Joel Vikre, is located in a historic warehouse building in the shadow of the Aerial Lift Bridge. Since its founding in 2012, Vikre has developed a diverse line of superb spirits made with Lake Superior water, but its flagship gins are still the distillery's calling cards. Boreal spruce, cedar, and juniper gins incorporate locally foraged botanicals, including, yes, Duluth spruce tips.

The distillery's cocktail room is a top destination: its Canal Park location makes it an easy find for thirsty tourists. Visit the Vikre website to add yourself to the waiting list so you can time your arrival appropriately. It's worth the wait for the privilege of enjoying some of the region's finest sipping just a few steps from the tanks where the magic happens.

525 S Lake Ave., 218-481-7401
vikredistillery.com

MORE COCKTAIL SHOPS

Dubh Linn Restaurant and Irish Brew Pub

This downtown Irish bar has a phenomenal whiskey selection.

109 W Superior St., 218-727-1559
dubhlinnpub.com

The Rathskeller

132 E Michigan St.
rathskellerduluth.com

The Tipsy Mosquito

Harking back to mid-century, this Two Harbors cocktail bar serves creative spins on vintage classics.

623 1st Ave., Two Harbors, 218-595-1174
thetipsymosquito.com

Zeitgeist Restaurant & Bar

222 E Superior St., 218-722-9100
zeitgeistarts.com/restaurant

7

WAIT IN LINE FOR BRUNCH
AT DULUTH GRILL BECAUSE IT'S WORTH IT

Generally speaking, visiting Duluth is a low-stress endeavor: you can go where you want when you want and it's not a problem. When it comes to brunch, though, you'll want to do some advance planning.

There's no buzzier brunch spot than Duluth Grill. On any given Sunday, you'll see its outdoor waiting area filled with fleece-wearing foodies, hockey-hair teens, and older couples ready to relax. They all come for the restaurant's leveled-up fare, which is only available at breakfast and lunch and those golden hours between.

Since breaking off from Embers in 2008, Duluth Grill has become the steady subject of national attention and local salivation. Stop by on impulse if you're patient or if it's not a prime weekend brunch hour; otherwise, use the restaurant's handy online queue function to grab a place in line and time your journey accordingly. You won't regret it.

118 S 27th Ave. W, 218-726-1150
duluthgrill.com

MORE BRUNCH STOPS

At Sara's Table Chester Creek Cafe

A neighborhood favorite with a focus on wholesome ingredients.

1902 E 8th St., 218-724-6811
astccc.net

Burrito Union

The hangover spot: for when you just want to smash your face into a breakfast burrito and maybe have a little hair of the dog.

1332 E 4th St., 218-728-4414
burritounion.com

Duluth Coffee Kitchen

Superb coffee and a well-crafted menu in the heart of downtown.

105 E Superior St., 218-221-6643
duluthcoffeecompany.com

Lake Avenue Restaurant

An elevated option, but not outrageously so . . . this is Duluth, after all.

394 S Lake Ave., 218-722-2355
lakeaveduluth.com

The Boat Club

For brunchers who really want to lean into the city's nautical flavor with a preppy atmosphere and a view of the lake.

600 E Superior St., 218-727-4880
boatclubrestaurant.com

8

WARM UP
WITH MIKE AND JEN'S COCOA

When you encounter a warm, sweet chocolate drink in Duluth, your host is apt to make a point of it if what you're drinking isn't just hot chocolate but Mike and Jen's Cocoa.

Mike and Jen aren't the cocoa's creators; they were its first taste testers. Duluth dad Dean Packingham invented the recipe so that his kids, Mike and Jen, could enjoy a product superior to mass-produced mix. Packingham and a friend, Amanda Cunningham, turned Mike and Jen's Cocoa into an entrepreneurial success story. The company prides itself on simple, natural ingredients that include whole milk powder, so you just need to add hot water. Delicious, wholesome, and practical. What could be more Duluth than that?

Mike and Jen's Cocoa is commonly served at eating and drinking establishments across Duluth, and the mix is stocked in numerous shops as well as available for online ordering. Check the company's website for specifics.

mikeandjens.com

9

BECOME A LOCAVORE
AT THE DULUTH FARMERS MARKET

The farmland in southern Minnesota is so rich, the northern part of the state can get short shrift when it comes to a reputation for freshly grown food. In fact, though, Northland farmers have been convening in Duluth for over a century to demonstrate that when it comes to quality agriculture, even the famed farmers of Iowa and Wisconsin shouldn't count their chickens.

Vendors at the Duluth Farmers Market, which is open regularly from May through October, typically sell a range of fresh produce as well as the likes of baked goods made with luscious local fruit; organic herbal tea; meat products (if you want a whole bison, you'll need to preorder); beeswax candles; coffee sold from a camper; and colorful flowers. Special events celebrate the harvest as well as holidays like May Day.

1324 E 3rd St.
duluthfarmersmarket.com

GO THE FULL MONTE
AT GRANDMA'S

Duluth is as nudity averse as the bracing weather and Midwestern culture would lead you to believe, but you can go "the Full Monte" by ordering an entire deep-fried Monte Cristo sandwich at Grandma's Saloon & Grill. It's just one item on a long menu of solidly prepared comfort foods.

Grandma's is about as close to a pure tourist trap as exists in Duluth, but even so, looking across the dining room you'll see a wide range of patrons: vacationers taking a breather, seniors treating themselves, construction workers enjoying the hearty fare. This restaurant is a local institution, synonymous with Duluth since its opening in 1976—when today's Canal Park was still regarded as "the warehouse district," replete with junky dumps that helped inspire the restaurant's antique-forward aesthetic.

522 S Lake Ave., 218-727-4192
grandmasrestaurants.com

TIP

Grandma's sometimes gets very busy, and it's easy to predict when: balmy summer weekend days during typical mealtimes. Try experiencing Grandma's as a cozy winter warmer—or, if you're hungry on a summer day, consider grabbing a snack and heading in for a late lunch or early dinner to beat the crowds.

11

RAISE A TOAST
TO DULUTH'S FIRST INDUSTRY AT FITGER'S

Before Duluth shipped ore or built airplanes, it brewed beer. Today, several new breweries continue that tradition of quality (see Discover "the Craft Beer Capital of Minnesota"), but if you want to go back to the beginning, step into the Fitger's complex.

August Fitger's brewery was a direct descendant of the city's first, established in 1859 on what is still called Brewery Creek. Fitger's ceased production in 1972, but the preservation-minded city kept the magnificent lakeside brewery building. It reopened in 1984 as a hotel and retail center, which it remains to this day.

Fitger's Brewhouse became the training ground for many of today's top local beer makers, and it's a popular spot to grab a bite and raise a pint brewed right there in the historic complex. The hotel provides classy lodgings with great views, and the many shops are a blast to browse.

600 E Superior St., 218-722-8826
fitgers.com

EAT BUZZWORTHY BBQ
AT OMC SMOKEHOUSE

Plenty of Duluth restaurants see summer crowds, but even on a gray February weeknight you'll find a hopping scene at OMC Smokehouse. A hub of Lincoln Park's burgeoning socializing and shopping scene, during peak season OMC can fill its entire courtyard with people waiting for tables.

What draws them? Delicious, consistent barbecued meat and a mouthwatering array of sides. The initials in the restaurant name stand for "oink, moo, cluck," and that pretty much tells you what you need to know about the varieties of meat that are nicely seasoned, perfectly cooked, and served with a choose-your-own caddy of sauces. In a nod to the Northwoods (and to practicality), maple is used for smoking. The results are successful enough that no less an authority than *Southern Living* magazine named OMC the Gopher State's go-to barbecue spot.

1909 W Superior St., 218-606-1611
omcsmokehouse.com

TIP

If you've placed an advance order online, you don't need to wait at the host stand. Just step into the restaurant and look for the shelf with orders ready for pickup.

13

LISTEN IN
AT DULUTH'S MUSIC MECCA: SIR BEN'S

Duluth is a small city with a huge music scene, and the heart of that scene is a quintessential local hangout: Sir Benedict's Tavern on the Lake. Located across the street from Fitger's and next door to the Kitchi Gammi Club, "Sir Ben's" is at once in the middle of everything and just a step off the beaten path.

An English-style pub, Sir Ben's is a go-to spot for everything from first dates to family sandwich stops to after-work drinks. The space may feel tight, but you'll be rubbing elbows with a happy crowd that includes more than its share of local musicians and music fans. All of Duluth's biggest names play Sir Ben's, which was famously the site of Trampled by Turtles' debut performance in 2003. During the Duluth Homegrown Music Festival, you may struggle to get in the door, but you'll be glad you did.

805 E Superior St., 218-728-1192
sirbens.com

TIP

If you're waiting in line to order sandwiches or salad, you don't have to stand empty-handed. You can step up to the bar and grab drinks to enjoy while you wait your turn at the sandwich counter.

14

MAKE A RESERVATION FOR DULUTH'S BEST PATIO

AT VA BENE

It doesn't sound like much, but "the Grotto" is Duluth's most spectacular dining patio experience. It's an open-air deck nestled beneath the lakeside Va Bene restaurant. The deck just has a few tables and a handful of lake-facing counter seats, so you'll want to plan ahead and make reservations: you can specifically request seating at the Grotto when it's open for the season. The deck has an extraordinary panoramic view of Lake Superior, the Lakewalk, and Canal Park—and the North Shore Scenic Railroad passes practically under your nose.

Oh, and the food's pretty darn good, too. Va Bene is popular year-round for its rich and enticing Italian food, served in a cozy setting that's a little elevated in comparison to most Duluth dining, but still unpretentious and accessible. Save room for gelato for dessert, or take a short after-dinner walk to the nearby Portland Malt Shoppe.

734 E Superior St., 218-722-1518
vabenecaffe.com

15

MAKE IT MEXICAN
AT OASIS DEL NORTE

If it's taco time, Duluth has you covered. There are solid Mexican food options downtown and in Canal Park, but Oasis Del Norte has earned a special place in the hearts (and stomachs) of locals and visitors alike.

Oasis Del Norte was launched in 2015 by Eduardo Sandoval Luna, who brought his family recipes from Mexico and started a food truck that became a mainstay of attractions, breweries, and special events. In 2023, the business finally landed a brick-and-mortar restaurant on Lincoln Park's main drag: West Superior Street.

With a range of options from tortas to burritos to walking tacos, Oasis Del Norte is ready to hit the spot for patrons looking to satisfy a south-of-the-border flavor craving. It's also a beloved community institution.

2401 W Superior St., 218-464-0824
oasisdelnorte.com

16

TAP A CIDER TWOFER
AT DULUTH CIDER AND WILD STATE

The more the merrier: that's the spirit when it comes to hard cider in Duluth, where two cideries thrive within a couple blocks of each other in the Lincoln Park neighborhood.

Between the two, Duluth Cider is slightly the elder, having opened in 2018. Owners Jake and Valerie Scott are UMD graduates who moved to the East Coast and discovered a cider culture they wanted to bring back to Minnesota. Their ciders put a distinctive spin on traditional techniques, and Duluth Cider frequently hosts live music at its cozy taproom.

Wild State Cider, opened in 2019, boasts a bright and spacious taproom with a large patio that's converted into a curling rink during the winter months. As its name suggests, Wild State has a somewhat more adventurous slate of cider flavors—and the taproom features an ice cream stand with Vermont-style soft serve.

Duluth Cider
2307 W Superior St., 218-464-1111
duluthcider.com

Wild State Cider
2515 W Superior St., 218-606-1151
wildstatecider.com

TIP

In 2023, the Duluth Entertainment Convention Center (DECC) launched an annual Cider North festival that's become a perennial hit, offering samples from a dozen-plus cideries in a playful indoor setting each winter. Watch the DECC's website and social media for announcements, and don't postpone grabbing tickets if you want to squeeze in!

17

JOIN A JUNETEENTH CELEBRATION

The rich history of Black Americans in Duluth includes pioneering notables like lodge proprietor George Bunga (namesake of nearby Bunga Township) and Janet Kennedy, who in 2023 became the first Black president of the Duluth City Council.

Each summer, Duluth joins the national celebration of Juneteenth: a holiday marking the end of slavery in the United States. The city's longest-running Juneteenth event is an annual cookout sponsored by the Duluth NAACP and held in the Central Hillside neighborhood. In recent years, an additional Twin Ports Juneteenth celebration has been held on both sides of the harbor.

In a somber coincidence, Juneteenth falls near the anniversary of a 1920 lynching that saw three Black men, falsely accused of rape, murdered by a mob. The Clayton Jackson McGhie Memorial in downtown Duluth hosts an annual event of remembrance.

Duluth NAACP Juneteenth Jubilee
Hillside Sport Court, 408 E 8th St.
duluthnaacp.org

Twin Ports Juneteenth
Duluth and Superior; specific location varies
facebook.com/twinportsjuneteenth

Clayton Jackson McGhie Memorial
Intersection of E 1st St. and N 2nd Ave. E, 218-336-2990
claytonjacksonmcghie.org

MORE ANNUAL EVENTS TO WATCH FOR

Homegrown Music Festival (Spring)
duluthhomegrown.org

Duluth Airshow (Summer or Late Spring)
duluthairshow.com

Rhubarb Festival (Summer)
chumduluth.org/rhubarbfestival

Sidewalk Days (Summer)
downtownduluth.com/sidewalk-days

Park Point Art Fair (Summer)
parkpointartfair.org

Art in Bayfront Park (Summer)
artinbayfrontpark.com

Northern Lights Music Festival (Summer)
northernlightsmusic.org

Duluth-Superior Pride (Labor Day Weekend)
duluthsuperiorpride.com

North Star Story Summit (Fall)
northstarstorysummit.org

18

DO COFFEE DOWNTOWN
AT DULUTH COFFEE

You may notice a trend among Duluth businesses: They don't have the world's most creative names. So many people have positive associations with the word "Duluth," businesses located here often feel there's no reason to think outside the box!

That brings us to the Duluth coffee company called—wait for it—Duluth Coffee Company. Since opening in 2012, the cozy shop has become a beacon for specialty coffee, and in 2023 the business expanded to offer a breakfast menu and café seating. There are other local craft roasters, and they're worth seeking out, but Duluth Coffee has claimed pride of place as the go-to spot for people in town who care about the quality of their joe.

Caffeine-loving visitors can bring a taste of Duluth home with them in the form of freshly roasted beans purchased directly at Duluth Coffee or from the coffee aisle of any local supermarket.

105 E Superior St.
duluthcoffeecompany.com

TIP

Watch for the St. Louis County Depot's annual Bienvenue Coffee Fest, a free fall event, to enjoy a generous taste of northern Minnesota's coffee culture.

SLIP INTO A SPEAKEASY
AT THE RATHSKELLER

Duluth is a city that loves to preserve its history, which means it has a lot of big old buildings with distinctive but tucked-away interior spaces ripe for reimagining. Thus there are any number of local drinking spots with what might be described as a "speakeasy" vibe, but the place that steers into it hardest is the Rathskeller: a cocktail bar and music venue in the lower level of Duluth's original City Hall.

The Rathskeller feels hidden because you have to step off the main drag of Superior Street and walk downhill to the parallel Michigan Street, where what's now a swanky nightspot was once a holding cell for the municipal court. Those 19th-century prisoners would be green with envy at what happens in the Rathskeller today: live jazz, seasonal cocktails made with spirits from near and far, and canoodling in the corner. What happens in Duluth . . .

132 E Michigan St.
rathskellerduluth.com

20

SATISFY YOUR SWEET TOOTH

Right next to the aptly named Duluth Coffee Company, you'll find the equally well-named Duluth Candy Co. This bright, cheerful shop stocks a variety of sweet treats with a specialty in popcorn mixes and fine chocolates. The shop is cozy and classic, but it's not old-timey: its clean packaging design nods to mid-century aesthetics.

You can also chase a sugar high in the close quarters of Hepzibah's Sweet Shoppe (in Canal Park's DeWitt-Seitz Marketplace). Then there's Sweetly Kismet Candy Store, in nearby Carlton, known for its sponsorship of an annual hot-air balloon festival.

If you're looking to head north, the Canelake family candy dynasty runs Canelake's Candies (a time-capsule candy store in Virginia, Minnesota) and Great! Lakes Candy Kitchen in Knife River (just up the North Shore). If you visit the latter location, be sure to explore the charming Bear Trail created by artist–chocolatier Patricia Canelake.

FIND YOUR SWEETS

Duluth Candy Co.

103 E Superior St., 218-481-7311
duluthcandyco.com

Hepzibah's Sweet Shoppe

394 S Lake Ave., 218-203-0058
chocolatesduluth.com

Sweetly Kismet Candy Store

1707 E Hwy. 210, Carlton, 218-460-9800
sweetlykismet.com

Canelake's Candies

414 Chestnut St., Virginia, 218-741-1557
canelakescandies.com

Great! Lakes Candy Kitchen

223 Scenic Dr., Knife River, 218-834-2121
greatlakescandy.com

21

DIVE INTO
A CLASSIC WATERING HOLE

Any harbor town worth its salt has some good dive bars—even if the water in that harbor is unsalted. When you're ready to go out wearing a Bulldogs hoodie instead of a blazer, Duluth's neighborhood hangouts are ready to welcome you.

Downtown, your options include Roscoe's Pioneer Bar, a spot in the shadow of City Hall where you can still occasionally overhear some choice conversations about the powers that be. Then roll down the hill to R.T. Quinlan's, which has a cave-like music space where you can hear some of the loudest shows in Duluth.

The real hub of Duluth dive bars, though, lies to the west. Duluth's expansive geography means you'll be catching a bus if you want to bar crawl, but it's worth it to hit distinctive spots like Curly's Bar, the Kom-On-Inn, and the Tappa Keg. Aren't you sold on the names alone?

TIP

Most places in Duluth take cards—and Bulldog hockey concessions have gone daringly cash-free—but you'll want to pack cash on your dive bar crawl.

DISCOVER THE DIVES

Roscoe's Pioneer Bar

323 W 1st St., 218-722-7100

R.T. Quinlan's

220 W Superior St., 218-722-3573
quinlansbar.com

Curly's Bar

2013 W Superior St., 218-727-9698

Kom-On-Inn

332 N 57th Ave. W, 218-624-3385

Tappa Keg Inn

7036 Grand Ave., 218-624-9881

The NorShor Theatre

MUSIC AND ENTERTAINMENT

22

GO LIVE
AT WUSSOW'S CONCERT CAFE

Live music at a coffee shop may not seem like a big deal, but Wussow's Concert Cafe isn't just any coffee shop. Owner Jason Wussow is a musician himself, playing with the popular ska band Woodblind, so he knows the Duluth music community as an insider. His namesake cafè opened in 1999 and has become an essential home for live music in Duluth. It's not huge, and that's part of the appeal: You'll be close to the music, whether you're seeing a seasoned local legend or a teen dreamer who's facing a crowd for the first time.

Wussow's has live music more nights than not, so chances are that no matter when you're ready to make your way to West Duluth, there will be a show you can take in. Whether or not it's showtime, the café serves a satisfying selection of drinks and seasonal eats.

324 N Central Ave., 218-624-5957
wussows.com

TIP

There's no need to wait for a special occasion to visit Wussow's, but the venue is particularly hopping during special series like the One Week Live recording sessions and the weeklong "Pete Fest" birthday celebration for doorman Pete Cich. Check the Wussow's website and social media for information on what's playing.

MORE MUSIC VENUES

Bent Paddle Brewing Co.

Popular brewery regularly hosts live music at indoor and outdoor stages.

1832 W Michigan St., 218-279-2722
bentpaddlebrewing.com

Earth Rider Brewery

Superior brewery maintains an active concert calendar with stages in bar-style taproom and outdoor "Festival Field."

1617 N 3rd St., Superior, 715-394-7391
earthrider.beer

Pizza Luce

Duluth location of Minnesota pizza chain turns into a rock club for regular live music shows.

11 E Superior St., 218-727-7400
pizzaluce.com/locations/duluth

23

BASK IN THE
BAYFRONT FESTIVAL PARK BREEZE

Bayfront Festival Park used to be a dump—literally. For most of Duluth's history, the harbor was primarily a working area, and the land just inside the Lift Bridge was home to junkyards and other artifacts of the city's industrial past.

That changed on July 4, 1985, when Bayfront Festival Park debuted. Today, Bayfront is widely regarded as Minnesota's best outdoor concert venue. Thousands of people fill the park for the shows by top touring acts and local heroes like Trampled by Turtles.

Normally, there's a festival of some sort at Bayfront every weekend from spring thaw through to early fall, after which volunteers begin the process of installing the spectacular Bentleyville holiday lights show. Even in the deep winter months, Bayfront remains active with ice-skating, saunas, and other activities. It's Duluth's most prominent, most awe-inspiring spot to enjoy entertainment and community.

350 Harbor Dr., 218-722-5573
bayfrontfestivalpark.com

24

CONTINUE A THEATRICAL TRADITION AT THE NORSHOR

The NorShor Theatre has lived many lives. Charlie Chaplin and the Marx Brothers played the theater in its first incarnation as the Orpheum. It was reconfigured to begin its life as the NorShor in 1941, a movie house that later fell into disrepair and became a strip club. A Herculean effort by the city and its partners restored the theater to glory and gave it to Duluth Playhouse, which keeps its stages and rehearsal areas busy throughout the year.

The NorShor main stage hosts Duluth Playhouse regular-season productions, often musicals, as well as the company's youth productions. A black-box space called the Lab hosts shows in the company's Underground series: more adventurous plays making use of the adaptable venue. The NorShor is also sometimes used for concerts and community events.

"This building," architect Matthew Janiak told *Architecture Minnesota*, "was brought back from the dead."

211 E Superior St., 218-733-7555
norshortheatre.com

CATCH
THE ZEITGEIST

While the NorShor Theatre may be the most visible landmark in Duluth's Historic Arts and Theater District, its neighbor across Superior Street does a lot of heavy lifting.

The Zeitgeist arts complex opened in 2009, when the NorShor was still a strip club. Today the neighborhood has turned around and Zeitgeist buzzes with theater, comedy, film, and visual art. Check out the calendar on any given week, and you may find a local painter's exhibit opening in the atrium, art house cinema on the two subterranean screens, an original production of a play, and improv comedy by the resident company.

Not only does Zeitgeist raise the bar for Duluth's arts scene, it supports the community with events and organizing. Not to mention, the cosmopolitan café serves diners and drinkers on their way to and from the parade of shows.

222 E Superior St., 218-722-9100
zeitgeistarts.com

FEAST YOUR EYES (AND ROLL UP YOUR SLEEVES)

AT THE DULUTH ART INSTITUTE

The Duluth Art Institute is one of the city's most venerable organizations, launched as a club in the late 19th century. Today, DAI supports the visual arts through a range of programming, including both exhibitions and classes.

Education programming is based in a former Carnegie library in the Lincoln Park neighborhood. Learners of all ages can work on drawing, painting, photography, ceramics, and other media—either in organized class settings or informal open studio opportunities, for artists who just want space and support.

The institute maintained gallery space in the Depot from the 1970s until 2024, when DAI's expertly curated shows of work by local and regional artists moved to a new location in the US Bank building downtown. Any art lover visiting Duluth should make a point of stopping by to see what's on display.

2229 W 2nd St. (education and studio space)
130 W Superior St., Suite 400 (gallery space)
218-733-7560
duluthartinstitute.org

27

ENJOY THE SOUNDS
OF THE DULUTH SUPERIOR SYMPHONY ORCHESTRA

The Duluth Superior Symphony Orchestra is one of the city's longest-standing cultural institutions, established in 1931. It offers an ambitious annual program of concerts featuring both classical music and pops shows, and its players can be heard in various configurations across the city.

The orchestra's main-stage season is set at the Duluth Entertainment Convention Center's Symphony Hall, an auditorium with a wide design that brings listeners close to the music. In addition to full-length evening concerts, the orchestra presents "casual concert" matinees with free admission for children.

In 2023, the orchestra moved its offices to the St. Louis County Depot, with access to the Depot Theatre for chamber music concerts and collaborations with musicians from other genres. Players from the orchestra also pop up at events like the Beer Garden happy hours at Great Lakes Aquarium. Wherever you find them, DSSO musicians are ready to sweep you away with accomplished artistry.

506 W Michigan St., Duluth (orchestra offices and Depot Theatre)
350 Harbor Dr. (Symphony Hall)
218-623-3776
dsso.com

TIP

The DSSO is far from the only option in town when it comes to classical music. Chamber ensembles and choral groups abound, and Lyric Opera of the North stages full-fledged opera performances. Duluth even has one of the world's leading handbell ensembles, Strikepoint. Check local entertainment listings for performances at venues like Sacred Heart Music Center, Weber Music Hall (UMD), and First United Methodist Church.

WATCH A MOVIE
MADE IN DULUTH

Duluth is far from Hollywood, but that's precisely the appeal for filmmakers looking for a distinctive setting and a welcoming community that, in recent years, has poured financial subsidies into its growing movie industry. If you're looking to relax in front of a screen, why not pick a movie that was made here?

Iron Will (1994) found a perfect spot for its sled dog story, while recent years' holiday rom-coms *Merry Kiss Cam* (2022) and *Rescuing Christmas* (2023) made magic in the Christmas City of the North—despite both being filmed during warmer months. If you can find it online, *You'll Like My Mother* (1972) is the perfect complement to a Glensheen visit. Patty Duke plays a young widow who gets trapped in a snowbound mansion with her mother-in-law (Rosemary Murphy), and cabin fever is the least of her worries.

TIP

Stay up to the minute on Duluth's movie industry by following the Upper Midwest Film Office online. Find them at:

uppermidwestfilmtv.org

POINT YOUR COMPASS
TO THE WEST THEATRE

The West Theatre has proved flexible, to say the least, since originally opening on Christmas Day 1937. (At one point, it even became a quilt shop.) Its current status as a venue for movies and live entertainment is thanks to local entrepreneur Bob Boone, who purchased and renovated the historic theater with an eye to its original art deco style.

Most typically, the West hosts first-run movies, making it a go-to stop for neighborhood residents who want to catch a flick without taking a trip downtown or up the hill. Often, though, the theater trades its movie screen for stage lights and hosts live music or other entertainment. You might be able to catch a local jazz group re-creating a classic album, a national touring act basking in the cozy atmosphere, or a comedian making dry remarks about the state of the world.

319 N Central Ave., 218-606-1211
thewesttheatre.com

READ A BOOK
WRITTEN, OR SET, IN DULUTH

Duluth has a vigorous literary scene, particularly strong in Indigenous voices and nature writing. Even writers who don't live here, though, absolutely love to write books that are set in Duluth. The combination of a vast lake and eerie Rust Belt industry makes the city a compelling setting for thrillers.

Every local bookstore has several shelves that are well laden with books written in or about Duluth. (See "Support an Independent Bookstore.") You might pick up one of Native author Linda LeGarde Grover's novels about love, loss, and memory. Or you might pick up one of Margi Preus's many books for young readers.

If you're looking for a page-turner, check out one of the crime novels starring Jonathan Stride, a Duluth police lieutenant dreamed up by Twin Cities author Brian Freeman. Or venture up the North Shore with *The Chuckling Fingers*, a vintage Agatha Christie-like whodunit by Mabel Seeley.

For more information on local literature:
lakesuperiorwriters.org

TIP

Famed author Gore Vidal wrote a novel named *Duluth*, but don't be fooled. The absurdist satire has virtually nothing to do with the actual Duluth.

31

GET STACKS OF WAX
AT RIVER CITY RECORDS & BOOKS

The name of River City Records & Books was inspired by a vintage sign that owner Todd Hanson found on sale along the Mississippi, but it's also apt for the store's Lincoln Park location: while the eastern portion of Duluth lies on Lake Superior, the western half lies along the St. Louis River estuary.

Arriving in 2023 to fill an important niche in Duluth's retail scene, River City has been embraced as the city's only brick and mortar store centered on records. The spacious, inviting shop also sells books and other media — need any VHS cassettes? The thoughtfully curated, well-organized selection is a blast to browse, so it's easy to lose an hour inside the store and emerge with a gleaming new release or a cherished golden oldie.

The front of the store also serves as a clearinghouse for flyers advertising concerts and other local events.

1814 W. Superior St., 218-464-1045
rivercityduluth.com

CATCH A RISING STAR ONSTAGE
AT UMD

Duluth visitors sometimes make the mistake of thinking that if they're past college age, the area's institutions of higher education don't have anything to offer. In fact, schools like the University of Minnesota Duluth (UMD) and the College of St. Scholastica offer lots for visitors to do and see—and you might even learn something.

UMD's Department of Theatre provides training for stage professionals both onstage and off, welcoming community members to a season of plays and dance performances at the Marshall Performing Arts Center. From Shakespeare to musicals, UMD students put their hearts and considerable talents into productions that are worth a trip "up the hill" to campus. Graduates have gone on to perform at professional theaters in Minnesota and beyond; catch these talented artists in Duluth so you can say you saw them first.

1215 Ordean Ct., 218-726-8562
cahss.d.umn.edu/departments/theatre

ENJOY THE SILENCE
AT WEBER MUSIC HALL

Weber Music Hall is likely to catch your eye before your ears start paying attention. It's an unmistakable landmark on the University of Minnesota Duluth campus, its egg-shaped copper roof rising above the treetops. Inside, daytime illumination comes from a 124-foot skylight stretching from front to back.

When the music starts, though, you'll be astonished by what you hear—and by what you don't. The hall, designed by Cesar Pelli and completed in 2002, is notable for its extraordinary sound insulation, making it even quieter than the Minnesota Orchestra's hall in Minneapolis. That makes Weber Music Hall perfect for the chamber music ensembles Duluth is increasingly known for.

The hall hosts a regular stream of concerts, typically open to the public (admission may be charged). That includes the annual Duluth Chamber Music Festival as well as other performances by both professional and collegiate groups.

1151 University Dr., 218-726-7361
cahss.d.umn.edu/centers-facilities/weber-music-hall

TAKE IN
THE TWEED MUSEUM

Duluth doesn't have a stand-alone art museum, but the University of Minnesota Duluth offers students and community members the opportunity to take in a wide range of superb regional, national, and international work at the Tweed Museum of Art. Although it's based at the university, the Tweed serves the public and is free to all visitors (donations are requested).

A two-story museum arranged around a central atrium, the Tweed hosts a range of rotating exhibits including work from its own permanent collection as well as outside work on temporary display—plus art by UMD students and faculty. The Tweed particularly prioritizes the display of Indigenous art; exhibitions are complemented by regular workshops, performances, and other programming.

With just over 9,000 square feet of exhibition space, the thoughtfully curated Tweed gives visitors a lot to look at.

1201 Ordean Ct., 218-726-8222
tweed.d.umn.edu

TIP

The Tweed also has a gift shop that's well stocked with prints, cards, and souvenir items. Its atrium lobby is a comfortable resting spot, featuring Duluth-made Loll all-weather furniture despite being insulated from the elements.

BEHOLD
MINNESOTA BALLET

People often cite the sprawling Homegrown Music Festival or the city's booming film industry as evidence of Duluth's strength in the arts, but they could just as well point to the superb professional ballet company making magic in a series of subterranean studios at the St. Louis County Depot.

Minnesota Ballet, founded in 1965, presents a full annual season of ballets. The company recruits talented dancers from across the country to perform in Duluth and teach classes for children and adults.

Like many ballet companies, Minnesota Ballet presents a *Nutcracker* each Christmas, but this one has a local spin: set at the Depot in the early 20th century, the Duluth Nutcracker substitutes show-off lumberjacks for leaping Russians and a snowball fight for a war against the rats.

506 W Michigan St. (office and studios), 218-733-7570
minnesotaballet.org

TIP

Every Minnesota Ballet performance is accessible to newcomers, so don't assume the big-story ballets are the only place to start. Smaller-scale performances at Studio Four bring you much closer to the dancers and allow a new level of appreciation for their art and technique.

GENUFLECT TO THE GROOVE

AT SACRED HEART MUSIC CENTER

The name of Sacred Heart Music Center is apt in two ways. First, it's a sacred space in the sense that it was built as a Roman Catholic church in the 1890s. It served that purpose for nearly a century before the building was sold and turned into a venue for music performance.

Second, the name fits because it's truly the heart of Duluth's music scene. Virtually every local artist of significance has played at Sacred Heart, with bands ranging from the iconic Low to the young synth duo embalmingEva considering it a special place. With the vaulted sanctuary remaining largely unchanged since its days hosting Mass, the historic building combines intimacy with majesty, a truly distinctive space to hear artists perform.

A nonprofit organization, Sacred Heart hosts shows throughout the year and is home to the Music Resource Center: a youth education program associated with the Duluth Armory.

201 W 4th St., 218-464-5464
sacredheartmusic.org

TIP

Since the COVID-19 pandemic began, Sacred Heart has become a local leader in offering live streamed and archived video of its shows. Check out the venue's YouTube profile to see what past and future performances are available.

GET ADVENTUROUS
ON THE INDIE ARTS SCENE

There are a lot of nooks and crannies in Duluth, both literally and figuratively. To experience the full richness of the city's arts scene, you'll want to get off the beaten path from time to time and find out what's happening in spaces where experimentation is the name of the game.

Past events by Duluth artists include an "art-infused church basement coffee and immersive psychedelic pancake feed dance party freak fest"; an appetizer hour with ASMR poetry whispering; and a piano on a floating platform passing beneath the Aerial Lift Bridge.

There's no centralized information hub for DIY events, but you can learn a lot by following local media—including social media. One independent publication with its ear to the ground is On the Record, a zine published by Duluth sound engineer Kristi Olson.

ontherecordzine.com

LISTEN LOCAL
WITH THE NORTH 103.3

The beloved "Antenna Farm" lining the top of Duluth's hill is evidence of the city's status as a regional broadcast hub, with an incredible amount of media compared to other metro areas of comparable size.

Minnesota Public Radio maintains a bureau and multiple broadcast signals in Duluth, but the radio station most firmly rooted in the city community is The North 103.3: a combination public radio, community radio, and college radio station that evolved from a 1956 project of the University of Minnesota Duluth broadcasting club.

Owned by PBS North (Duluth's public TV station) since 2021, The North 103.3 has a schedule that, at varying times, features regular professional music hosts, community volunteers playing specialty shows, and college students playing . . . well, college music. Tune in to get a direct ear on what Duluthians of all ages are talking about and listening to.

103.3 FM (broadcast signal), 218-726-7181
thenorth1033.org

TIP

If podcasts are more your speed, just search your favorite platform for "Duluth" and you'll discover a wealth of options. Just make sure the podcast you pick is about Duluth, Minnesota—not Duluth, Georgia.

GET A READ
ON THE DULUTH PUBLIC LIBRARY

The downtown Duluth Public Library may not be long for this world. It's not particularly energy efficient, and its striking design has proved challenging to adapt for the community's changing needs. As of this writing in 2024, city leaders are considering a range of options that may involve replacing the structure entirely.

While it's there, though, check it out! The 1980 building was designed to evoke the shape of an ore boat and the color of a foggy day on Lake Superior. While many Duluthians have never felt the library's clean modern lines fit with the more ornate architecture of its neighboring buildings, the blog *Perfect Duluth Day* calls it "arguably the most significant building to be built in Duluth in the past 80 years."

It's also a warm gathering space that does what it was designed to do: hold books and other materials for community use.

520 W Superior St., 218-730-4200
duluthlibrary.org

TIP

The Duluth Public Library system also maintains well-appointed branch locations in West Duluth and at the Mount Royal Shopping Center.

CUDDLE UP
AT MARCUS THEATRES

When you're ready for a movie break in Duluth, you don't have far to go. In addition to the art house cinema downtown (see "Catch the Zeitgeist"), Duluth has a first-run movie theater operating within the harborside DECC complex. There's something quintessentially Duluth about going to see the latest superhero movie or historical epic, then stepping out the theater door and seeing a massive freighter (the retired *William A. Irvin*) stretching out before you.

The DECC movie theater is run by Marcus Theatres, a Midwestern chain that encourages patrons to bring blankets for that extra cozy factor. Don't be surprised, when you're standing in line for popcorn, to see patrons of all ages walking past you looking like they're ready for a night on the couch at home. If your movie nights include adult beverages, there are plenty of options available in the stylish Movie Tavern.

300 Harbor Dr., 218-722-1573
marcustheatres.com/theatre-locations/duluth-cinema-duluth

TIP

Because the Marcus theater is part of the DECC complex, there's a charge to enter the parking lot. If you purchase movie tickets in advance, though, you can flash your confirmation receipt for free parking.

Aerial Lift Bridge
Credit Visit Duluth

SPORTS AND RECREATION

EXPERIENCE SAUNA
WITH CEDAR + STONE

If all you know of sauna is sitting in a tepid wood-paneled room next to a hotel pool, get ready to have your mind blown. In Duluth, sauna is serious business.

First, you'll want to pronounce it *sow-na*, first syllable rhyming with "now." That's the Finnish way. Sauna is the word for both the heated chamber ("I never want to leave this toasty sauna") and the experience ("We shared good sauna today, friend").

Now that you've mastered the lingo, there's really no wrong way to sauna. In Duluth, you're apt to stumble over a sauna anywhere from the street (a rolling sauna) to the lake (a floating sauna) to a basement (a private sauna). If near Lake Superior, a cold plunge is recommended to complete the sauna experience.

If you need a place to start, check out Cedar + Stone, a local company that maintains beautifully crafted public saunas.

Cedar + Stone Sauna Experience
800 W Railroad St.
cedarandstonesauna.com/experience

42

HIT THE BEACH
AT PARK POINT OR BRIGHTON

Duluth is a beach town, and it's so easy to admire the majesty of Lake Superior from just about anywhere that visitors often forget they can hop right in. Anytime!

A stunning sandy beach runs along the length of Minnesota Point, also known as Park Point and home to free city parks. Just cross the Aerial Lift Bridge and make your way to the beach house at the end of the point. Or, if you're feeling impatient, snag a space just across the bridge at Franklin Square.

For a completely different Duluth beach experience, try the rocky Brighton Beach at the eastern end of the Lakewalk. Standing on the jagged basalt formation, you'll know you're not at Cape Cod. The adjoining Kitchi Gammi Park, also run by the city, includes a picnic area that makes a fine spot for lunch on the lake.

Park Point: 4750 Minnesota Ave.
Franklin Square (12th Street Beach): 1200 S Lake Ave.
Brighton Beach (Kitchi Gammi Park): 7030 Congdon Blvd.
218-730-4300
duluthmn.gov/parks

HIT THE TRAILS
ON TWO WHEELS

Thanks to varied topography and a trail network that's seen substantial investment in recent decades, Duluth specifically and northeastern Minnesota generally have emerged as an international hot spot for mountain biking. There are also plenty of paved trails, if you'd prefer a slightly less adventurous experience.

The City of Duluth maintains no fewer than six different mountain bike trails, ranging from the beginner's trail at Hartley Park to the more challenging Piedmont and Brewer trails and the heavily sloping Spirit Mountain experience. If you're ready to go the distance, the 42-mile Duluth Traverse runs the city's entire ridgeline.

Information on trail locations, conditions, and etiquette is available from both the city and from the nonprofit organization Cyclists of Gitchee Gumee Shores. Local bike shops can get you set up with rental or purchase equipment, and there are also classes and skills clinics for riders who need a refresher.

Duluth Parks
duluthmn.gov/parks

Cyclists of Gitchee Gumee Shores
coggs.com

SLIDE INTO WINTER
ON A PAIR OF SKIS

Yes, Duluth has a steep hill—and you know what that's good for! Among many ways to get active outside during the Northland's long months of winter wonderland, you can go downhill skiing without even crossing the city limits.

Spirit Mountain is an unmistakable landmark above West Duluth, with 22 alpine runs for downhill skiing and snowboarding. The runs are well maintained and offer enough variety to challenge beginners through intermediate skiers. The facility also features a range of other downhill pursuits, including snow tubing and mountain biking. The Adventure Park has rides, including an alpine coaster and a bench-style zip line.

If you prefer cross-country skiing, you can do that at Spirit Mountain, too. Alternately, there are groomed trails at several city parks, with equipment rentals available at local shops and selected on-site facilities. The Duluth Cross-Country Ski Club has all the information you need to get moving.

Spirit Mountain
9500 Spirit Mountain Pl., 800-642-6377
spiritmt.com

Cross-country ski trails at Duluth parks
duluthmn.gov/parks/trail-pages-list/cross-country-ski-trails

Duluth Cross-Country Ski Club
duluthxc.com

PICK UP
A PADDLE

Whether you prefer a kayak, a canoe, or a paddleboard, Duluth offers many distinctive opportunities to propel yourself through its scenic waterways. Of course, sometimes the waterways propel you. Duluth lends itself to a more active sort of paddling than you'll get on the placid surface of Minnesota's 10,000 *other* lakes. You don't need to be a whitewater daredevil, but embracing the adventure is encouraged.

If you have your own equipment, there are many places to put in—including Duluth's harbor, as long as you keep a safe distance from the working vessels. Multiple companies offer kayak or canoe tours, and Zenith Adventure can set you up to explore the city's marquee waterways. You can even take a Rise & Ride tour to see the sun rise as you paddle under the Aerial Lift Bridge and out into the lake.

Lake Superior State Water Trail
dnr.state.mn.us/state_water_trail/virtual_tour/
lake_superior/snapshot.html

Zenith Adventure
323 Harbor Dr.
zenithadventure.com

TIP

If you'll be spending some time in the area, you can learn whitewater paddling in the comfort and safety of an indoor pool at the University of Minnesota Duluth, where pumps create artificial turbulence. Find information at umdrsop.d.umn.edu/aquatics.

46

TREK ALONG
THE SUPERIOR HIKING TRAIL

Duluthians' coffee tables commonly have well-thumbed copies of the *Superior Hiking Trail Guidebook*. The 300-plus-mile trail winds its way along the North Shore, from the Wisconsin border south of Duluth up nearly to the Canadian border above Grand Marais. It couldn't be easier to access; it winds right through Duluth itself, including a section along the Lakewalk.

That makes it easy to check this one off, if that's all you want to do—but if you enjoy a good walk in the woods for an up-close encounter with the Northland's natural wonder, take an extended hike either along the trail through Duluth or somewhere else along its length. There are plenty of spots to hop on, and the trail passes through several state parks.

You don't even need a guidebook; the Superior Hiking Trail Association maintains a detailed website with maps and updated information about trail conditions.

218-834-2700
superiorhiking.org

MORE HIKING TRAILS

Mesabi Trail

150 miles of paved trail running through the Iron Range

111 Station 44 Rd., Eveleth (trail office), 877-637-2241
mesabitrail.com

Minnesota Point Pine Forest Scientific Natural Area

Park Point trail featuring old-growth pine and excellent bird-watching

218-300-7871
dnr.state.mn.us/snas/detail.html?id=sna02000

Quarry Park

Half-mile trail at a Duluth quarry that's often used for ice climbing in the winter

1325 N 59th Ave. W, 218-730-4300
duluthmn.gov/parks/parks-listing/quarry-park

Waabizheshikana: The Marten Trail

Trail showcasing views of the St. Louis River

7300 block of Grand Ave., 218-730-4300
duluthmn.gov/parks/parks-listing/
waabizheshikana-the-marten-trail

Willard Munger State Trail

70-mile trail running between Duluth and Hinckley, with views of forests, lakes, and wildlife

7261 Pulaski St. (northern terminus), 651-296-6157
dnr.state.mn.us/state_trails/willard_munger/index.html

47

GET INTO
A REAL PICKLE(BALL) GAME

The international phenomenon known as pickleball has been embraced in Duluth, and locals aren't going to let a little snow stop them. The Duluth Indoor Sports Center—acronymically known as the DISC—is a bubble rising out of the Northwoods, reached by driveway off Rice Lake Road in the hilltop Kenwood neighborhood.

Even the most avid pickleballers can satisfy their cravings at the DISC, which offers open play several days a week. The regulars are serious about their games, but also friendly and welcoming to players of all experience levels. Courts are also available at local spots, including parks and YMCAs.

When you're ready to take your game to the next level, the Duluth Area Pickleball Association connects players and supports tournaments. The DISC and other facilities also host tennis matches for those who like their courts a little larger.

Duluth Indoor Sports Center
4402 Rice Lake Rd., 218-722-0810
discmn.com

Duluth Area Pickleball Association
duluthpickleball.org

48

WADE INTO
A DULUTH HUSKIES BALL GAME

Sure, Duluth is known as a winter sports town, but this is still the Midwest and it wouldn't be a proper summer without enjoying the national pastime. Both veteran baseball fans and newcomers to the spectator sport—including kids—will be charmed by Duluth's historic Wade Stadium. Built in 1941, the venue evokes the spirit of a simpler time. A view, past the left field foul line, of ore cars on an elevated rail supplying the CN dock will help remind you what city you're in.

Wade Stadium is home to the Duluth Huskies, playing in the Northwoods League against rivals like the La Crosse Loggers and the Thunder Bay Border Cats. Catching the Huskies won't break the bank, and it will help restore your love of the game.

101 N 35th Ave. W, 218-786-9909
duluthmn.gov/parks/parks-listing/wade-stadium
northwoodsleague.com/duluth-huskies

THROW A ROCK
AT THE DULUTH CURLING CLUB

As you would expect, Duluth is an international hub of curling: the Olympic sport that involves sliding heavy stones (or "throwing rocks," in curling parlance) down a sheet of ice, with teammates who furiously "sweep" the ice to strategically ease friction.

The Duluth Curling Club has been home ice to champions including Team (John) Shuster, gold medalists at the 2018 Winter Olympics. By membership, it's the second-largest curling club in the United States (following another Minnesota curling club, in St. Paul). Flags and victory banners festoon the club and its cozy barroom, located in the harborside DECC complex. The club offers how-to events for beginning curlers as well as leagues and bonspiels (tournaments) for players who've found their footing.

If you just want to take a peek before setting out, all eight lanes at the club are continuously live streamed on YouTube. And, yes, people do watch.

327 Harbor Dr., 218-727-1851
duluthcurlingclub.org

TIP

The Duluth Curling Club is technically a private club, meaning you can't just walk in anytime unless you're a member, but the organization encourages anyone curious about curling to learn more. Contact the club if you're interested in stopping by to see what all the excitement is about.

50

ROOT FOR THE BULLDOGS
AT AMSOIL ARENA

Bulldogs, the animals, don't have anything in particular to do with Duluth. The University of Minnesota Duluth sports teams are named after a well-jowled UMD football player in the 1930s.

The Northland is all about hockey, though, and with no pro team nearer than St. Paul, college and prep pucks are closely watched. The city's premier sporting events are UMD hockey games, played at Amsoil Arena (part of the Duluth Entertainment Convention Center). Both the women's and men's teams are national powers, so the chances you'll see a win are good.

The arena seats fewer than 7,000 fans in a hockey configuration, so games frequently sell out; plan ahead and reserve your seats. Visit the UMD Bookstore on campus to properly outfit yourself in maroon and gold, the colors of the University of Minnesota system.

350 Harbor Dr., 218-722-5573
decc.org

WALK (OR RUN OR BIKE OR SCOOTER)

THE LAKEWALK

Superior Street may be Duluth's central commercial corridor, but what's that street named after? Yep, people want to be near the lake. That makes the Lakewalk a de facto main street for tourists, commuters, and people of all ages who want to spend some time enjoying the changing moods of "Mother Superior."

There are many ways to traverse the Lakewalk, an eight-mile paved trail running along Lake Superior from the Aerial Lift Bridge to Brighton Beach. Strolling, bicycling, and skating are all popular ways to enjoy the stretch—as are the motorized scooters that are available to rent from multiple vendors.

For a statelier form of transportation, you can rent a surrey (a four-wheel pedal-powered conveyance) or take a ride in a horse-drawn carriage. Wheel Fun Rentals (wheelfunrentals.com) has bikes, and when available you can catch a carriage from Top Hat Carriage Service (tophatcarriages.com).

600 Canal Park Dr. (Lake Superior Marine Visitor Center, at the west end of the Lakewalk)
218-730-4300
duluthmn.gov/parks/parks-listing/lakewalk

TAKE A CHANCE
AT FOND-DU-LUTH CASINO

Here's something you can do in Duluth that you can't do in any other Minnesota city: visit a downtown casino.

Fond-du-Luth opened in 1986, the result of a major effort designed to help generate economic activity that was then badly needed by both the city of Duluth and the Fond du Lac band of Lake Superior Chippewa. In a special arrangement authorized by the federal government, Fond-du-Luth became Minnesota's only casino built on land not part of an existing tribal reservation.

Converted from a former Sears building, Fond-du-Luth isn't elaborate as far as casinos go. You can count on lots of slots and a varying selection of other games. Still, it scratches the itch for casino buffs, and it's worth the visit for the novelty value alone. For better or for worse, it's not quite as novel as one other concept considered in the '80s: putting a bingo hall inside the *William A. Irvin*.

129 E Superior St., 218-720-5100
fondduluthcasino.com

53

PLAY IT COOL
WITH LAKE SUPERIOR KUBB

Northlanders pronounce the name of the game with a hard K and a long U. It's a Swedish lawn game that involves throwing short wooden rods ("batons") at the opposing team's row of rectangular blocks ("kubbs"). If your team is the first to topple your opponents' kubbs, you get to go for the king standing tall in the center.

There's more to it than that, but it's basically a yard game with a little more personality and local color than just throwing beanbags at boards. The notion that kubb is descended from a Viking pastime is a bit of a stretch, but it's fun to imagine.

Kubb is also fun to play, and the organization Lake Superior Kubb brings the game into the community at events ranging from the Lake Superior Ice Festival to casual events at parks and Earth Rider Brewery.

lakesuperiorkubb.com

TIP

When you're ready to invest in your own set, numerous stores across Duluth have kubb blocks available for sale.

54

RUN
GRANDMA'S MARATHON

No, the apostrophe in that heading isn't a typo. Grandma's Saloon & Grill is a Canal Park landmark, but it's become best known for sponsoring one of the country's most picturesque marathons. Grandma's Marathon, which takes place each June, has won raves among runners for its stunning lakeside setting and a level of professional organization that belies the relatively small size of its host city.

A qualifying race for the US Olympic Trials and the Boston Marathon, Grandma's is one of the country's 10 largest marathons and requires some advance planning if you're hoping to run the course: Check the race website for registration details and grab a ticket immediately when availability begins. A half-marathon and a 5K are available for less advanced runners, and you can feel the excitement at every level.

351 Canal Park Dr. (business office), 218-727-0947
grandmasmarathon.com

TIP

Grandma's weekend is a great party for spectators as well. All are welcome to join runners in a ticketed spaghetti dinner at the Duluth Entertainment Convention Center and for free entertainment in Bayfront Festival Park.

55

DROP A LINE
IN THE LAKE

Fishing is a way to connect closely with Duluth's crystal waters—whether in the Great Lake or in nearby streams and rivers.

Minnesota's Department of Natural Resources maintains a helpful guide to fishing spots in the area, as well as information on fish prevalence and state regulations. Between the city's abundant streams, inland lakes, and of course the Big Pond itself, it's not hard to find a tempting spot to try your luck. Multiple local charter companies will take your group out onto Lake Superior for an unforgettable angling experience.

Of course, some local fishers would say that dropping a line only when the surface is liquid is taking the easy way out. Ice fishing is a quintessential northern Minnesota experience, but it shouldn't be attempted without proper equipment and full knowledge of the ice conditions. The DNR can help there, too.

dnr.state.mn.us/areas/fisheries/duluth/index.html
dnr.state.mn.us/gofishing/learn-ice-fish.html

GET DEEP
WITH A LAKE SUPERIOR DIVE

The infamous "underwater hotel" dreamed up by a former mayor of neighboring Two Harbors never came to be, but there are much less science-fictional ways of seeing below the surface of Lake Superior.

Experienced divers love the Great Lake for its clear water, distinctive terrain, and rich history. Yes, that means shipwrecks—and charter companies like Sol Mates help divers find stunning sights all along the lake shore, from the North Shore to the Apostle Islands.

The lake presents its challenges for divers, though, and professionals are available to help you get up to speed, whether you're new to scuba diving or just new to Duluth. Charter companies typically provide classes as needed, and Lake Superior Divers Supply and School offers a range of general and specialty classes. If you've only seen Lake Superior from the surface, after all, you're missing most of it!

Sol Mates Boat Charters
99 Beach Dr., Silver Bay, 651-208-9277
solmatesboatcharters.com

Lake Superior Divers Supply and School
3028 W 3rd St., 218-624-7285
lakesuperiordivers.com

57

CATCH A WAVE

Of all Duluth's big-water attractions that seem remarkable for Minnesota—diving underwater, moving mountains of ore, riding a cruise ship—none is more incongruous than surfing. Is it really possible to ride the curl on the Unsalted Sea?

It sure is. Lake Superior surfers have to layer up a bit compared with their peers in California or Hawaii, but the pastime is so popular that Duluth even has a surf shop. Step into the Back Alley and you'll feel like you're in a Beach Boys song, especially after you get charged up at the coffee counter.

If you need more than just a board, surfing lessons are available through private instructors and through the University of Minnesota Duluth. Duluth locations, including Park Point and Stoney Point, are considered among the best surfing spots on Lake Superior. What are you waiting for?

The Back Alley
2409 W Superior St., 218-464-1786
backalleysurf.com

UMD Recreational Sports Outdoor Program
Sports and Health Center, 1216 Ordean Ct., 218-726-7128
umdrsop.d.umn.edu

SET SAIL
OFF PARK POINT

With its stunning vistas and crisp winds, it's no surprise that Lake Superior is a mecca for sailors. On Wednesday nights from mid-May through mid-September, the Duluth Yacht Club organizes sailboat races just outside Duluth Harbor, where the speeding vessels can be clearly seen from much of the city.

The area has numerous marinas for sailors to dock their boats and access resources, but if you're just getting started behind the sail, there's a place for you too. The Duluth Superior Sailing Association, based on the harbor side of Park Point (technically, Minnesota Point), offers lessons for curious sailors of all ages to learn the basic skills required to operate a sailboat. The organization even provides small boats, and when your skills are strong enough you can borrow one to chart your own course.

Of course, charters are also available from private operators if you'd prefer to let someone else do the work!

Duluth Yacht Club
duluthyachtclub.com

Duluth Superior Sailing Association
5025–5041 Minnesota Ave.
sailingforall.org

GET GAMING
AT THE LOCH

As incredible as Duluth's natural wonders are, the long winter months have taught locals to use their imaginations for escapes to distant worlds. At the Loch, that means gathering around game boards and building community while battling dragons. The shop's name nods to Loch Ness, a body of water that can evoke mystery and wonder akin to Lake Superior.

The Loch is a coffee shop and gaming haven that opened in 2023: an inviting two-story space in a charming brick building. Inside, owners Matt and Erin Glesner invite visitors to grab a coffee, pull up a chair, and stay awhile. Visitors can bring their own games or shop from the selection available for sale. The shop hosts regular events for both novice and experienced gamers, so however many experience points you've earned you can find a spot at the Loch.

318 N 18th Ave. E, 218-606-1104
facebook.com/thelochcafeduluth

TIP

Game players and comic fans will also want to check out Rogue Robot Games & Comics (downtown Duluth) and Collector's Connection (in Miller Hill Mall).

BECOME BETTER
AT BOCCE

The game of bocce has long been popular in northern Minnesota, a favorite pastime of the European immigrants who worked the mines of the Iron Range. It was a passion project of the late Rudy Perpich, Minnesota's only governor to hail from the Range, who aspired to build bocce courts across the state.

In Duluth, as you might expect, opportunities abound to play the game in which players toss large colored balls as close as possible to a smaller "jack." Skyline Social & Games hosts summer leagues featuring a fast-paced version of the game—or, for a slightly slower and more traditional experience, the Duluth Bocce League hosts games at the city's Wheeler Athletic Complex.

"I haven't met a person [who] doesn't enjoy the game," said Duluth Bocce League organizer Dave Campanario, who cited one regular player being 93 years old. "Anybody can play."

Skyline Social & Games
4894 Miller Trunk Hwy., 218-727-8555
skylinesocialandgames.com

Duluth Bocce League
3501 Grand Ave. (court location), 218-724-4643

TAKE TO THE AIR
WITH FLY DULUTH

Even from high atop Enger Tower, it's impossible to appreciate the full scope and variety of Duluth's 80-plus square miles. Fortunately, it's possible to get a true bird's-eye view of Lake Superior's busiest port.

Fly Duluth offers a range of scenic flight tours over the city, including a romantic Sweetheart Tour, a nighttime City of Lights Tour, and a Duluth/Superior Tour featuring both sides of the state line. A Discovery Flight is oriented less toward the scenery than toward the mechanics of powered flight, enabling passengers to get a sense of whether flying is something they might like to pursue themselves.

If your interest is piqued, the organization offers a range of flight training classes that allow students to pursue a pilot's license or other certifications. Need to rent a plane? They can help with that, too.

4535 Airport Approach Rd., 218-461-0520
flyduluth.com

TIP

While hot-air balloons rarely fly over Lake Superior, due to the difficulty of controlling them amid the big-water weather, the candy store Sweetly Kismet hosts an annual balloon festival just south of Duluth in Carlton.

BECOME A
BIRD NERD

It's not only humans who like to pass through Duluth: The area's unique geographic location and wide range of environments makes it a perfect place to spot birds. The Northeastern Minnesota Bird Alliance hosts events, recommends hot birding spots, and generally supports nature conservation in the area.

One notable spot to bring your binoculars is Duluth's Hawk Ridge Bird Observatory, a global destination for birders who want to observe raptor migration. It's an important site not just for amateur gawkers but also for organized research into the movements of raptor populations.

Then there's the Sax–Zim Bog, a rich preserve among the northern Minnesota peatlands that's known as "the Arctic Riviera" for its hospitality to cold-weather species. As a wintering area for hawks and owls, the bog affords fascinating spotting opportunities year-round and hosts a January event billed as "the world's coldest birdathon."

Sax–Zim Bog
8793 Owl Ave., Toivola, 218-209-2266
saxzim.org

Northeastern Minnesota
Bird Alliance
nemnbirdalliance.org

Hawk Ridge Bird Observatory
(best observation locations vary by season)
3980 E Skyline Pkwy., 218-428-6209
hawkridge.org

CHOOSE YOUR COMPETITION
AT SKYLINE SOCIAL

Despite its name, Skyline Social & Games is not an establishment you patronize for the view. That's okay, because at this Miller Trunk Highway emporium your attention won't be on what's out the windows.

This large complex is full of opportunities for friendly competition. In addition to standard bowling lanes, Skyline is the only northern Minnesota spot with lanes for the cuter, more unusual pastime of duckpin bowling. If you're looking for the kind of league sport that involves having a drink in your hands either during or shortly after the match, Skyline has your hookup: their leagues and tournaments include volleyball, bowling, bean bag throwing, axe throwing, the regionally popular sport of bocce, and even cribbage.

Plus, Skyline has an arcade—with a prize counter. How's your Skee-Ball arm?

4894 Miller Trunk Hwy., 218-727-8555
skylinesocialandgames.com

GET PICKY
AND GO ICE CLIMBING

If you really want to drop the mic when your friends ask how you spent your time in Duluth, make sure your answer includes the words "climbed a wall of ice." Quarry Park is named for the former use of a site that now, thanks to past excavations, boasts a hundred-foot-high sheer cliff that often coats with ice during the wintertime. Ice farmers work to help the process along, and the park has become a nationally known destination for those who find plain old rock climbing to be a little, well, pedestrian.

Climbing that cliff may seem daunting, but as is typical for Duluth, experienced athletes are eager to share their interest with newcomers. The Duluth Climbers Coalition offers clinics and serves as an information hub, while the company Vertical Endeavors sells gear-included ice climbing experiences.

Quarry Park
1325 N 59th Ave. W, 218-730-4300
duluthmn.gov/parks/parks-listing/quarry-park

Duluth Climbers Coalition
duluthclimbers.org

Vertical Endeavors
329 S Lake Ave. (Duluth location), 218-279-9980
verticalendeavors.com/outdoor-ice/ice-lessons

PLAY A MINI-GOLF COURSE LIKE NONE OTHER

If you want a classic, kitschy miniature golf experience in Duluth, complete with a final hole that has you putt your ball into a model of Enger Tower, Canal Park's Adventure Zone has you covered. If you're looking for a truly distinctive mini-golf layout, though, make your way to Spirit Mountain's Adventure Park. There, you'll find a miniature golf course designed by lauded local architect David Salmela.

When you hire a lauded architect to design your mini-golf course, don't expect gnomes and windmills. For starters, Salmela's course isn't green; it's black. Yes, black—with white obstacles. It runs along a single continuous track, raised off the ground and punctuated with short gatelike passages. At a glance, you might mistake it for a war memorial. Why such an unexpected approach? Salmela wanted to do something different, and Duluth is a town where exactly that kind of thing can happen.

9540 W Skyline Pkwy., 218-628-2891
spiritmt.com

The Depot

CULTURE AND HISTORY

CELEBRATE
THE CHRISTMAS CITY OF THE NORTH

General Waverly, the *White Christmas* innkeeper, should have set up shop in Duluth: There's relatively little suspense as to whether "the Christmas City of the North" will be under a blanket of snow come December 25.

Duluth goes big for the holidays. Thousands of visitors come each year to enjoy distinctive shops, festive attractions, and special traditions like the region's cherished Tom and Jerry cocktail.

It all kicks off at the Christmas City of the North Parade, typically held the Friday before Thanksgiving. Once Santa makes his appearance on Superior Street, it's open season for holiday fun, including Bentleyville, one of the country's largest free holiday lights displays. In recent years, local artists have mounted a "Boubville" installation with skewed takes on the city's more wholesome holiday attractions. There's no wrong way to do Christmas in Duluth.

700 Railroad St. (Bentleyville, at Bayfront Festival Park)
bentleyvilleusa.org

TIP

If you want to pick up a tree while in Duluth, make your reservations early for the unforgettable Christmas Tree Train, run by the North Shore Scenic Railroad. The train departs the St. Louis County Depot and rolls to Knife River, where passengers select their trees from a lot and the evergreens are tossed onto a flatbed car for the ride back to Duluth. There are also nearby tree farms if you prefer to cut your own.

HUNT FOR GHOSTS
IN CANAL PARK

From Lake Superior shipwrecks to murder inheritance plots, Duluth is teeming with opportunities for ghosts to be spawned and to stick around. If you're curious about the supernatural—or just enjoy a good ghost story—you've come to the right place.

Kimberly Christine, an experienced phantom hunter who's appeared on the Travel Channel's *Ghost Adventures*, leads three-hour tours through Canal Park from June through October. Christine shares historical tales and clues visitors in to where ghosts might be lurking; the tours even include opportunities to conduct tests using equipment like electromagnetic frequency detectors.

One of the area's supposedly most haunted spots is the *William A. Irvin*. Tours of the retired freighter are available through the summer, and in October it becomes a "Haunted Ship" attraction, where you're guaranteed to meet some ghouls.

Duluth Ghost Tours
323-843-8688
duluthghosttours.com

William A. Irvin
350 Harbor Dr., 218-722-5573
decc.org/william-a-irvin

GLORY
IN GLENSHEEN

The historic house known as Glensheen, built by Chester and Clara Congdon in the early 20th century for their large family and numerous staff, sits on a stunning piece of lakeside property with a formal garden, a creek, and outbuildings. It's been open to the public under the management of the University of Minnesota Duluth since shortly after the 1977 death of the Congdons' last surviving child, Elisabeth.

Tragically, that death was part of an infamous double murder, part of an inheritance plot that continues to fascinate locals and visitors. You can read more about that in any of several books, but you don't need to be a true-crime obsessive to enjoy the well-maintained mansion and relax on its comfortable grounds. To visit Glensheen is to step through a window back in time to when Duluth was at the zenith of its wealth and power.

3300 London Rd., 888-454-4536
glensheen.org

TIP

Glensheen is gloriously decorated for the holidays, in the spirit of the Congdons' Christmas celebrations. On weekend nights from late November until New Year's, the mansion typically offers candlelight tours to see the trees and lights in all their evening splendor.

DO A DAY
AT THE DEPOT

The St. Louis County Depot has been a local landmark since 1892, when it was built as a union station. While its neighbor, the Soo Line Depot, was demolished in 1972, the building today's Duluthians simply call "the Depot" survived to become an arts and cultural heritage center.

The marquee attraction is the Lake Superior Railroad Museum, one of America's best transportation museums. You can explore the museum's densely packed collection of stationary trains and ride the associated North Shore Scenic Railroad, with excursions up the shore, including on seasonal specialty trains.

Elsewhere in the Depot, you'll find historical exhibits, Minnesota Ballet's Studio Four performance space, the Depot Theatre, and fascinating surprises tucked into the building's many nooks and crannies. While there are admission costs to visit the railroad museum, ride the trains, and see certain shows, most of the Depot is free and open to the public.

506 W Michigan St., Duluth, 218-733-7571
experiencethedepot.org

TIP

Check the Depot's website and social media for free special events ranging from model train demonstrations to craft coffee fairs to movie marathons. You're also welcome to just grab a seat in the stately Great Hall and relax while you plan your next Duluth adventure.

GET INTO THE SWIM
AT GREAT LAKES AQUARIUM

Since opening in 2000, Great Lakes Aquarium has become one of Duluth's destination attractions, particularly for families with children. There are plenty of animals to look at—from those as common as a crow to those as exotic as an octopus—but the aquarium is also designed with many interactive elements.

Kids can steer boats through a model of the Great Lakes (complete with locks) and enjoy up-close encounters with fish in a touch tank. There's even a dedicated play area for young children. What's more, all ages can enjoy the views of Duluth Harbor. The aquarium is easily accessible via walkway from Canal Park, and the outdoor equipment at Playfront Park is nearby.

For art lovers, a hidden gem of the aquarium is the Merrill Lynch Art Gallery, the world's only such gallery dedicated to rotating displays of local art at an aquarium facility.

353 Harbor Dr., 218-740-3474
glaquarium.org

TIP

If you're planning to be in Duluth more than once a year, a membership to Great Lakes Aquarium or Lake Superior Zoo is worth considering. A membership to either one accords discounted admission to the other, as well as benefits at other zoos and aquariums across the country.

BE ENCHANTED BY GREYSOLON,
DULUTH'S SIGNATURE BALLROOM

Grand hotels were marks of distinction for cities in the early 20th century—and Duluth was not going to be left behind! When the Hotel Duluth opened in 1925, locals were convinced they had the most beautiful such building in the country.

The former hotel rooms have been converted to apartments, but the communal spaces remain as works of grandeur that are popular for meetings and celebrations, most particularly weddings. The Black Woods Group now rents a street-level dining room decorated in Moorish Revival style, as well as the 3,780-foot Greysolon Ballroom, with its richly detailed surfaces and chandeliers that would impress even the Phantom of the Opera.

While the spaces aren't open to the public daily, occasional ticketed events—concerts, holiday meals—allow visitors to enjoy the Roaring Twenties majesty, even if no one's getting hitched.

231 E Superior St., 218-722-7466
greysolonballroom.com

TIP

Get excited for your Greysolon visit by checking out the historic hotel lobby and Moorish Room as seen in the movies *Iron Will* and *Merry Kiss Cam*.

CHECK THE SITCH
AT THE KITCHI GAMMI CLUB

There's a reason this book isn't called *100 Things to Do in Duluth Right This Minute.* Getting inside the Kitchi Gammi Club may take a little planning, but it's worth the wait.

"The Kitch," as locals call it, prides itself as being the oldest incorporated club in Minnesota. Founded in 1883 as a means for Duluth's elites to rub elbows above the fray, the club has been based since 1913 in a striking neo-Gothic building located just across East Superior Street from the big lake.

It's still a private club, so becoming a member is the ultimate way to enjoy the club's Arts and Crafts interior with its extensive spaces for dining, drinking, and relaxing. It's not a place where you can just casually pop in, but the Kitch does host regular open houses for the public to take a peek: Watch the club's social media for details.

831 E Superior St., 218-724-8589
kitchigammiclub.com

TIP

Many Duluth groups and organizations host functions at the Kitchi Gammi Club. If you're able to stick around town and keep your eyes open, you can ultimately see plenty of the Kitch. If you find yourself repeatedly drawn to its doors, maybe that's a sign that it's time to inquire about membership.

FOLLOW THE BEACON

TO SPLIT ROCK LIGHTHOUSE

Okay, that's easier said than done . . . the Split Rock Lighthouse beacon is rarely illuminated, most reliably on the November 10 anniversary of the sinking of the *Edmund Fitzgerald*. Fortunately, you can easily find the historic site without a bright light: It's just up Highway 61.

Split Rock is one of the most recognizable lighthouses on the Great Lakes, even earning a cameo in Baz Luhrmann's *The Great Gatsby*. Built in 1910 and active until 1969, the lighthouse is now run by the Minnesota Historical Society for visitors to learn more about Lake Superior's maritime history and enjoy the remarkable North Shore views. A museum and educational programs bring the site alive, with occasional special events if you can time your visit for a special ceremony like the *Fitzgerald* commemoration. An adjacent state park offers further opportunities to explore the shore, including Minnesota's own "Pebble Beach."

3713 Split Rock Lighthouse Rd., Two Harbors, 218-226-6372
mnhs.org/splitrock

USE DULUTH'S MOST POPULAR BATHROOM

AT THE LAKE SUPERIOR MARITIME VISITOR CENTER . . . THEN, SEE A SHIP

The Lake Superior Maritime Visitor Center is much more than a place to relieve yourself, but that's why it exists. The US Army Corps of Engineers decided to add a second story to a planned public restroom, and the result became one of Duluth's most-visited museums.

The free facility contains a wealth of information about the history of shipping on the Great Lakes, with interactive displays and models—yes, including a model of the wreck of the *Edmund Fitzgerald*. The park rangers on staff are full of information about topics including the next ships expected to pass under the adjacent Aerial Lift Bridge.

There's nothing like the awesome spectacle of seeing a massive freighter squeeze through the Duluth Ship Canal, and the visitor center can provide you with all the information you need to make a sighting during shipping season, which runs through all but the dead of winter.

600 Canal Park Dr., 218-788-6430
lsmma.com

TIP

Wondering what ships are hanging out on the lake? This is the era of GPS, so multiple websites can identify boats with names and other information. Google "Lake Superior ship tracker" and take your pick.

75

SEE THE STARS—
INSIDE OR OUT

One advantage of being far from big-city lights is that Duluth and its environs offer remarkable stargazing, with regular opportunities to spot the northern lights. A trip up the North Shore or to Voyageurs National Park will take you even farther into dark-sky territory, but there's plenty to be seen within the city as well.

To orient yourself, make a visit to the Marshall W. Alworth Planetarium at the University of Minnesota Duluth. Staff present regular programs that include tours of the current night sky, along with deeper dives into topics such as black holes and the nature of our sun.

The Arrowhead Astronomical Society hosts certain planetarium shows and holds regular meetings and telescope viewing events. Their website also collects useful information for those interested in taking a closer look at the Northland night sky.

Marshall W. Alworth Planetarium
1023 University Dr., 218-726-7129
scse.d.umn.edu/marshall-w-alworth-planetarium

Arrowhead Astronomical Society
duluthaas.com

GET INSIDE A LAKER:
THE *WILLIAM A. IRVIN*

In Great Lakes shipping parlance, a "laker" is a freighter that stays within the lakes, while a "saltie" is a freighter that passes through the St. Lawrence Seaway to reach the open ocean. Most of the ships you'll see in Duluth are examples of the former, which are larger because their size isn't limited by the need to pass through all those locks.

That includes the *William A. Irvin*, a 611-foot boat launched in 1937 and retired in 1978—an older contemporary of the *Edmund Fitzgerald*. While the *Irvin* doesn't have the bells and whistles of today's bulk freighters, the basic configuration hasn't changed, so touring the *Irvin* is a can't-miss opportunity for anyone curious about how these big ships work.

Permanently moored in Minnesota Slip, the *Irvin* is open for public tours from late spring through early fall, when the freighter transforms into Duluth's "Haunted Ship."

The *William A. Irvin* is part of the Duluth
Entertainment Convention Center
350 Harbor Dr., 218-722-5573
decc.org/william-a-irvin

77

ENJOY THE VISTA (FLEET)
ON A HARBOR CRUISE

Why just stand there and look at the water when, instead, you can be out on it? The Vista Fleet's boats, the *Vista Queen* and the *Vista Star*, provide easy and highly enjoyable opportunities to see Duluth from the lake, the harbor, and the St. Louis River.

The fleet offers a wide range of excursions, with the classic standby being the Duluth Waterfront Tour. The 75-minute cruise takes you out into the harbor and under the Aerial Lift Bridge—you'll feel like royalty—to see the city from Lake Superior itself.

There's also a longer Grand Sightseeing Tour as well as special excursions to spot fall colors, enjoy Independence Day fireworks, and hear live music. Only some of the cruises involve full meals, but snacks and drinks (both alcoholic and nonalcoholic) are generally available for purchase on board.

323 Harbor Dr., 218-722-6218
vistafleet.com

TIP

Vista Fleet season passes are available for regular riders. Subscribe to the fleet's email newsletter for notifications and potential discounts.

CLIMB TO THE TOP
OF ENGER TOWER

It's understandable that most visitors miss some of Duluth's "hidden gems." What's harder to understand is how many people miss Enger Tower, an 80-foot stone observation tower visible from much of the city.

The 1939 edifice is named in tribute to Bert Enger, the Norwegian immigrant businessman who donated a swath of hilltop land to the city of Duluth to be enjoyed in perpetuity by the entire community. Two generations of Norwegian royalty have participated in dedication ceremonies at the tower, which stands strong even as the winds whip off Lake Superior.

Open seasonally from May 1 until the first snowfall, the five-story tower provides a breathtaking view of the city and its surrounding landscape, including the vast freshwater lake stretching out to the horizon. Visiting in 2011, Norway's King Harald V told Minnesota Public Radio, "I can easily see why so many Norwegian immigrants decided to settle here."

1601 Enger Tower Dr., 218-730-4300
duluthmn.gov/parks/parks-listing/enger-park

TIP

While you're visiting Enger Tower, take time to visit the rest of the park, with paths that connect to the Superior Hiking Trail. The park also has copious picnic table seating and a seasonal food vendor.

PLAY ALL DAY
AT THE DULUTH CHILDREN'S MUSEUM

Located in an unassuming Lincoln Park building, the Duluth Children's Museum keeps a relatively low profile that belies its impressive history. Founded in 1930, it's one of the country's oldest children's museums, and it's jumped around a lot: Gen-Xers might remember playing in the museum's former St. Louis County Depot space.

Today the cultural artifacts that families once came to peer at are tucked away in storage, and the museum's emphasis is on active play. A Cirrus airplane, representing one of Duluth's most successful companies, is the centerpiece of a main floor that includes ample play equipment and rotating exhibits that engage young visitors in hands-on learning. A separate space ensures that babies and toddlers have safe room to play without being trampled by older kids.

The museum also offers regular workshops as well as special holiday events like the Noon Year's Eve bash, with its countdown to 12:00 p.m.

2125 W Superior St., 218-733-7543
duluthchildrensmuseum.org

MORE SPOTS FOR KIDS TO PLAY

Great Lakes Aquarium

One of local families' favorite rainy-day spots.

353 Harbor Dr., 218-740-3474
glaquarium.org

Lake Superior Railroad Museum

Kids love to run through this museum and explore the many train cars and engines they're permitted to enter.

506 W Michigan St., 218-727-8025
lsrm.org

Lake Superior Zoo

Lots of trails and exhibits to enjoy, with playground equipment for young children.

7210 Fremont St., 218-730-4500
lszoo.org

Playfront Park

Public park with play equipment for kids, part of Bayfront Festival Park.

700 W Railroad St., 218-730-4300
duluthmn.gov/parks/parks-listing/bayfront-festival-park-playfront-park

Ursa Minor Brewing

Spacious craft beer taproom also serves pizza, with play area for kids. A great lunch option when young ones need room to roam.

2415 W Superior St., 218-481-7886
ursaminorbrewing.com

TAKE THE
RIVER TRAIN

Understandably, Duluth is known as a lake city. However, it's not just situated alongside Lake Superior; it's also on the lake's US headwaters, the St. Louis River. As the river runs into Lake Superior, it produces one of America's largest freshwater estuaries. For the best view of that remarkable ecosystem, hop a train.

Not, in this case, the North Shore Scenic Railroad. That runs north along the lakeshore. The Lake Superior and Mississippi Railroad, known locally as the "River Train," follows the first train route to reach Duluth. The River Train is slower and less flashy than the busier Scenic Railroad, but the river ride is an unforgettable experience for patient, curious riders. Along the line you'll see historic industry, a former steel plant site being reclaimed for parkland, and some of the teeming flora and fauna along the river.

6930 Fremont St.
duluthrivertrain.com

TIP

Be sure to venture out onto the open-air Safari Car when rolling along the Mud Lake causeway, which rides so low that the train seems almost to be directly on the water's surface.

81

EMBARK
ON A GREAT LAKES CRUISE

Large cruise ships, once a common sight on the Great Lakes, became scarce for decades—but recently, travelers have again taken interest in exploring the inland seas on majestic new vessels. The return of cruise ships to Duluth has been exciting for both visiting passengers and the locals who welcome them.

Typically, cruises on Lake Superior make Duluth a port of call, meaning that passengers visit and may disembark in the Zenith City but their journeys begin and end elsewhere. Occasionally, though, Duluth is a port of origin, where passengers begin cruises such as a 2023 Viking Polaris trip that began in Duluth and went all the way to Antarctica.

Joining a Lake Superior cruise through Duluth is a significant investment and takes advance planning, but passengers report that the experience of riding a full-size cruise ship under the Aerial Lift Bridge is second to none.

Cruise the Great Lakes (information service)
cruisethegreatlakes.com/ports/duluth-minnesota

CRASH IN A TRAIN STATION
AT THE ENDION INN

With Duluth's booming tourist industry, short-term rental properties have been popping up all over. One has particular interest, though, for people who want to stay by the lake and also appreciate the city's rich history as a rail hub.

Built in 1899 as a passenger depot for the Duluth & Iron Range Railroad, Endion Station is a marvel in red brick and sandstone, a monument to Duluth's burgeoning wealth and influence at the turn of the 20th century. The station was moved to Canal Park when Interstate 35 came through in the 1980s, and today it serves as the Endion Inn.

With just five rooms, the Endion Inn provides a distinctive way to stay in a comfortable spot that also holds a piece of Duluth's history, within earshot of the Great Lake's crashing waves. Plus, there's a community sauna. What's more Duluth than that?

200 Lake Place Dr., 218-591-5875
endioninn.com

TIP

Railroading fans will also be interested in the Northern Rail Traincar Inn, a Two Harbors establishment where each room is situated in a retired boxcar.

MORE SPOTS TO STAY

Fitger's Inn

When it comes to historic character, it's hard to beat this converted brewery, a tourism landmark for decades.

600 E Superior St., 218-722-8826
fitgers.com

Enger Lofts Hotel

These airy rentals are located in the trendy Lincoln Park neighborhood.

1832 W Superior St., 218-203-0606
engerloftsduluth.com

Pier B Resort

The perfect spot to stay if you're planning to catch an attraction at Bayfront Festival Park.

800 W Railroad St., 218-481-8888
pierbresort.com

Edgewater Hotel & Waterpark

Two words: water park.

2400 London Rd., 218-728-3601
duluthwaterpark.com

South Pier Inn

If you really want to get up close and personal with the Aerial Lift Bridge, there's no better spot. When a ship comes through, you'll know it.

701 S Lake Ave., 218-786-9007
southpierinn.com

DO THE
LAKE SUPERIOR ZOO

The Lake Superior Zoo is off the beaten path compared to the attractions in Canal Park and downtown Duluth, but it's well worth making your way out west to explore this lovely landmark, cherished by locals and visitors for over a century.

Situated in a spacious but secluded piece of former parkland with a creek winding through it, the Lake Superior Zoo offers the opportunity to get up close and personal with animals both familiar and exotic, while knowing you're supporting conservation and responsible care at the Association of Zoos and Aquariums–accredited facility. In recent years the zoo has been shifting its emphasis toward showcasing animals comfortable in Duluth's cold-weather climate, although temperature-controlled buildings still contain certain species native to jungles and deserts.

The relaxed, kid-friendly zoo offers organized classes and even has a school on-site. It's open year-round, with a different experience every season.

7210 Fremont St., 218-730-4500
lszoo.org

TIP

Look for "Mr. Magoo," the now-taxidermied mongoose who became a local legend in 1963. Gifted to the zoo, he was facing death or deportation due to a prohibition on mongooses—enacted due to fear that they would establish themselves as an invasive species, threatening birds and other native animals. After vigorous public debate, Magoo was officially pardoned by the John F. Kennedy administration and allowed to live out the remainder of his life in the zoo's custody.

SEE THE CUTTING EDGE
OF AVIATION AT CIRRUS

Planes take a back seat to boats and trains in Duluth's public image, but one of the city's most important, innovative companies produces vehicles bound for the sky. Cirrus is the world's largest producer of general aviation aircraft—in other words, private planes.

There's a reason Cirrus, based in Duluth since 1994, comes out on top. Its planes have a range of nifty features, but the most astonishing is the parachute packed into each craft. In the case of emergency, a Cirrus plane can deploy a parachute to safely shepherd the entire intact aircraft to a soft landing. According to the company, the technology has saved more than 250 lives.

Purchasing a Cirrus plane takes a serious investment, but anyone can visit the Duluth factory and see how the company's equipment is made. The company offers tours on Wednesdays at 1 p.m., with advance reservations required.

4515 Taylor Cir., 218-727-2737
cirrusaircraft.com

TIP

The annual Duluth Airshow is a can't-miss event for aviation buffs. Check duluthairshow.com for details on each year's show, which typically takes place in the summer or late spring.

PAY HOMAGE TO PAVEMENT
AT GRANITOID MEMORIAL PARK

Never to be outdone in transportation infrastructure, Duluth prides itself on having Minnesota's oldest stretch of concrete pavement. In fact, a two-block section of East Seventh Street has the second-oldest intact stretch in the United States.

In perhaps the ultimate example of Duluthians' frequent drives to preserve the city's historic character, a group of locals campaigned to preserve the concrete when the streets were being repaved in 2000. There's even a small, triangular park—the suitably named Granitoid Memorial Park—paying tribute to the pavement, which was a technological innovation when it was originally installed in 1909–10. Scored with lines to help horses' hooves find traction, "Granitoid" was a patented surface.

Today, resident Carolyn Sundquist told the *Duluth News Tribune*, the heavily patched Granitoid forces drivers to slow down and, whether they like it or not, appreciate the history beneath their tires.

Intersection of N 25th Ave. E and E Seventh St.
(Granitoid Memorial Park)

E Seventh S between N 26th Ave. E and Wallace Ave.
(original Granitoid surface)

longviewgardenclub.wordpress.com

86

MAKE A
BOB DYLAN PILGRIMAGE

A range of great musicians have come from, or come through, Duluth—but one stands alone. Bob Dylan, the most revered songwriter in American history and the only popular musician to win the Nobel Prize in Literature, was born in Duluth on May 24, 1941. He only lived in the city for a handful of years before his family moved up to the Iron Range city of Hibbing, but any list of Duluth distinctions must include being the origin of the boy born under the name Robert Zimmerman.

Dylan's actual birthplace was St. Mary's Hospital, since replaced by a newer building. His first home is easy to find, though, and fans can join an annual front-lawn concert celebration on the legend's birthday. Another essential spot is the Duluth Armory, where a teenage Dylan had a formative experience watching Buddy Holly perform live.

Duluth Dylan Fest (annual celebration)
duluthdylanfest.com

Bob Dylan childhood home (private home not open
to the public, but may be seen from the exterior)
519 N 3rd Ave. E

Duluth Armory (currently closed while under renovation)
1301–1305 London Rd., 218-464-0227
dulutharmory.org

TIP

Both of Dylan's parents, as well as both of his paternal grandparents, are buried in Tifereth Israel Cemetery in Rice Lake—just north of Duluth. The shared gravestone of his parents, Beatrice and Abram Zimmerman, is typically piled with stones as fans, family, and friends honor the deceased per Jewish tradition.

Lake Superior Art Glass

SHOPPING AND FASHION

SHOP
CANAL PARK

Duluth's most concentrated shopping neighborhood is also its tourism epicenter: Canal Park, named for the Duluth Ship Canal passing under the Aerial Lift Bridge. Gifts, apparel, art, and antiques are among the items on offer at dozens of shops within easy walking distance.

Strolling along Canal Park Drive, you can't miss the boutiques and souvenir shops, with many more available inside the DeWitt-Seitz Marketplace just around the corner on Lake Avenue. Whether you're looking for a cozy shacket, a print by a local artist, a fun puzzle, or a T-shirt proudly declaring "I'VE BEEN TO DULUTH" (as seen in the movie *The Great Outdoors*), Canal Park is full of products curated with lakeside pride.

Canal Park is also the place to grab a bite, ride a horse-drawn carriage, and enjoy attractions like the Lake Superior Maritime Visitor Center—not to mention dip a toe into the lake itself.

Duluth Visitor Center is in
Grandma's Saloon & Grill,
in the heart of Canal Park
522 S Lake Ave., 218-722-4011
visitduluth.com

MORE SOUVENIR STOPS

UMD Bookstore

If you want to represent for Duluth's most avid sports fandom, grab your Bulldogs swag here.

1120 Kirby Dr., 218-726-7286
umdstores.com

Lincoln Park

Numerous shops are all within walking distance of each other, tilting toward craft rather than crap.

1800–2100 W Superior St., 218-727-6573
(Lincoln Park Business Group)
lpbg.org

Lake Superior Railroad Museum

If you need a souvenir for a rail fan in your life, this is the spot, with items representing a dazzling array of trains past and present.

506 W Michigan St., 218-727-8025
lsrm.org

Great Lakes Aquarium

The "Explorers' Cove" shop sometimes seems like a bigger draw than the fish and particularly caters to kids.

353 Harbor Dr., 218-740-3474
glaquarium.org

The Bookstore at Fitger's

All of Duluth's indies have literary-minded gift items. This one has the benefit of being in a shopping mall.

600 E Superior St., 218-727-9077
fitgersbookstore.com

MEET THE MAKERS
IN THE LINCOLN PARK CRAFT DISTRICT

The Lincoln Park Craft District isn't an official designation. It's a brand that companies in the Lincoln Park neighborhood came up with to highlight the fact that in the 2010s independent makers of quality goods began to cluster there.

Today the district is an essential stop for Duluth visitors and a regular hangout for locals. You can start your stroll through the shopping area with some caffeine from 190° Coffee and Tea, one of several merchants in the highly Instagrammable Enger Lofts building. For happy hour, there are three breweries, two cideries, and a fine whiskey selection to accompany the mouthwatering food at OMC Smokehouse.

Other highlights include Frost River (packs and outdoor gear), Damage Boardshop (skate gear), and Zenith Basecamp (gifts and apparel in a "glamping" hostel with wine bar). Along the way, treat yourself to a scoop or two from Love Creamery.

Superior St. between W 18th Ave. and W 27th Ave.
Find a map at ecolibrium3.org/lincolnpark

TIP

Lines can be long at Lincoln Park's popular eating spots. If you're hoping to eat sooner rather than later, try ordering ahead online and grabbing a pickup order to bring to one of the neighborhood's breweries or cideries.

89

GET FIT
AT DULUTH TRADING COMPANY

Duluth Trading Company is not quite as local as its name might lead you to believe. It's a publicly traded company with dozens of stores across the US, and its flagship store is located at its current home base of Mount Horeb, Wisconsin. That said, there is still a very nice Duluth Trading Company retail location in the store's namesake city.

The company got its start in Duluth in 1989. It was originally named Portable Products and focused on gear for the construction industry. The company's peak Duluth moment came in the early 1990s, when it was located on a barge and the business adopted its current name. After the company moved away in 2000, its comfy clothing became hugely popular . . . and the rest is history.

Today in the company's Duluth store you'll find a generous selection of the products that have helped make the city's name synonymous with unpretentious quality.

300 E Superior St., 218-481-7580
duluthtrading.com

SPEND A DAY
IN GRAND MARAIS

As Duluth is to Minneapolis, Grand Marais is to Duluth: a delightful destination just a bit farther into the Northwoods, a little bit cozier with Lake Superior. Grand Marais is a spot you may pass through on your way to the Boundary Waters or Grand Portage, but it's worth a stop in its own right to experience the inspiring Artists' Point and enjoy the sight of the iconic harbor.

The city also has plenty to offer shoppers. Several shops sell local art and crafts, and you can outfit yourself for adventure at the Lake Superior Trading Post. Joynes Ben Franklin offers a classic dime-store experience. Drury Lane Books is a readers' paradise: a cozy independent shop right on the lake. When you're ready to take a break, queue up at Java Moose Espresso Café, Voyageur Brewing Company, the harborside Angry Trout Café, or the landmark Gunflint Lodge.

visitcookcounty.com/places-to-visit/grand-marais

TIP

Although Grand Marais enjoys a summertime surge, most shops and restaurants are open year-round. Make a wintertime visit for dramatically reduced lodging rates and shorter lines with the same exceptional products and service—not to mention, the evocative ice effects where water meets land.

MORE DAY TRIP DESTINATIONS

Castle Danger Brewing

Northern Minnesota's largest craft brewery by volume, Castle Danger is one of many attractions in the North Shore city of Two Harbors.

17 7th St., Two Harbors, 218-834-5800
castledangerbrewery.com

Madeline Island Ferry Line

Bring your car or bike—or just walk on—for a ride to the largest Apostle Island from the charming town of Bayfield.

20 Washington Ave., Bayfield, 715-747-2051
madferry.com

Soudan Underground Mine Tours

The deepest underground mine tour in the United States.

1302 McKinley Park Rd. (summer entrance),
Soudan, 218-300-7000
dnr.state.mn.us/state_parks/
lake_vermilion_soudan/tours.html

Bob Dylan Childhood Home

See the house and city where the music legend spent his school years after his family moved from Duluth.

2425 7th Ave. E, Hibbing, Private home
hibbingmn.gov/217/bob-dylan-walking-tour

Judy Garland Museum and Children's Discovery Museum

Step inside the screen star's childhood home and see artifacts from her career, including the Emerald City carriage from *The Wizard of Oz*.

2727 S Pokegama Ave., Grand Rapids, 218-327-9276
judygarlandmuseum.com

91

GO OVER THE HILL
TO MILLER HILL MALL

Duluthians can debate the city's planning and layout for days—bring up the Interstate 35 extension if you really want to start a conversation—but it's hard to argue with the convenience of Miller Trunk Highway.

That unromantic name describes the strip of Highway 53 heading northwest out of Duluth, along which you'll find a wide variety of chains, car dealerships, and big-box retailers. While the area is as car oriented as you'd imagine, a city the size of Duluth was bound to develop that kind of corridor, and its location keeps it out of sight from the city's more picturesque neighborhoods. At the same time, it's close to the city and easy for residents to visit on errands.

Miller Hill Mall is the area's signature shopping attraction. While other malls of its vintage (1973) have faded, this one remains a favorite hangout for Duluthians looking for a little retail therapy.

Miller Hill Mall
1600 Miller Trunk Hwy., 218-727-8301
simon.com/mall/miller-hill-mall

92

SUPPORT AN INDEPENDENT BOOKSTORE

Duluth has a well-earned reputation as a place where people like to get outdoors, but the city's majestic winters also provide some of the coziest vibes imaginable for curling up with a good book while you let it snow, snow, snow.

The city's independent-minded residents fiercely support independent bookstores, and readers are covered both east and west. The Bookstore at Fitger's is situated in the historic brewery complex overlooking Lake Superior from the East Hillside neighborhood, while Zenith Bookstore is at the hub of a growing culture scene in West Duluth's Spirit Valley neighborhood.

If you love digging through well-loved books in search of a special find, check out Amazing Alonzo, an Endion neighborhood shop that still attracts the kind of rabid readers who think Kindles are for the birds.

The Bookstore at Fitger's
600 E Superior St., 218-727-9077
fitgersbookstore.com

Zenith Bookstore
318 N Central Ave., 218-606-1777
zenithbookstore.com

Amazing Alonzo
1831 E Superior St., 218-724-3431
amazingalonzobookstore.com

93

STROLL
SUPERIOR STREET

References to being "Superior" abound all along the shore of the greatest Great Lake—including in Duluth's sister community of Superior, Wisconsin. It's only natural, then, that Duluth's main drag should be called Superior Street.

Superior Street takes on a different character as it passes through numerous neighborhoods in the city, including the up-and-coming Lincoln Park neighborhood west of downtown. It's in the heart of the city, though, that Superior hums with the hustle and bustle of a historic commercial district. Take the time to walk east from Duluth Public Library to Leif Erikson Park, and along the way you'll see everything from theaters to shops to restaurants to the newsroom of the local paper of record. Like all American downtowns, Duluth's is a zone of constant change and frequent challenge, but it's always been core to the town still claiming the title of the Great Lakes' "Zenith City."

TIP

Downtown Duluth is also the name of the business association in the city's commercial core. Its website and social media are full of information about events and specials, and it sponsors free events including Movies in the Park. Learn more at downtownduluth.com.

94

OUTFIT YOURSELF FOR ADVENTURE
IN EAST HILLSIDE

If you've arrived in Duluth without the proper gear for an outdoor experience—or if you'd simply like to upgrade your equipment—the city has no shortage of spots to set you up.

A good place to start is at the historic Fitger's complex in the East Hillside neighborhood. The store Trailfitters has all the layers of clothing you'll need to get outdoors in comfort and safety, whether you're just taking a casual hike or embarking on something more ambitious.

If your adventure includes a bike, skis, snowboard, or even paddles, you can head a few blocks up the hill to Ski Hut or Continental Ski and Bike. Either business can get you set up for snow sports or biking, with some rental options if you're not ready to make a permanent commitment. Check their websites or call ahead to check availability.

Trailfitters
600 E Superior St., 218-722-6776
trailfitters.com

Ski Hut
1032 E 4th St., 218-724-8525
skihut.com

Continental Ski and Bike
1305 E 1st St., 218-728-4466
continentalski.com

EXPERIENCE INDIGENEOUS FOOD AND CRAFT

AT AICHO

The American Indian Community Housing Organization was founded in 1993, "created as an Indigenous response to social conditions in Duluth, MN, powered by the urban Native American community," as its website states.

While the organization first saw to basic needs like food and shelter, AICHO (AY-ko, as locals pronounce the acronym) has since expanded its programming to encompass a wide range of services, activities, and community actions. That includes frequent art exhibits and makers' markets in and around AICHO's headquarters just a couple blocks up from the center of downtown Duluth.

Watch AICHO's website and social media for notices of markets around holidays as well as outdoor food and art markets in the summer. The organization hosts exhibits of Indigenous art year-round, typically opening with receptions featuring refreshments and opportunities to meet the artists.

202 W 2nd St., 218-722-7225
aicho.org

96

LOLL-Y-GAG
IN DULUTH'S SIGNATURE ALL-SEASON FURNITURE

You don't need to spend much time in Duluth before you start to notice a ubiquitous form of furniture: plastic, monochrome, all-weather chairs and tables in trim geometric designs. That's Loll furniture, and in recent years it's become one of Duluth's most iconic exports—seen everywhere from Harvard's campus to Pacific Northwest island gardens. In Duluth itself, the locally manufactured furniture is everywhere. Loll's material, which can stand up to even the most extreme Duluth weather, is made from recycled milk jugs.

While Loll's West Duluth production facility doesn't have a showroom, the company itself recommends you visit Bent Paddle Brewing, where Loll furniture fills both indoor and outdoor spaces and you can get a good sense of how it looks and feels. If you're ready to invest in a piece or two for yourself, the company's website offers the company's full line for shipping or pickup.

5912 Waseca St. (preorder pickup only), 877-740-3387
lolldesigns.com

SHOP THE SWEET SELECTION
AT HUCKLEBEARY

While Duluth's gift shops are largely concentrated in Canal Park, it's worth making a detour downtown to visit the charming Hucklebeary on Superior Street—easy to reach via pedestrian bridge from Gichi-ode' Akiing (Lake Place Park) on the Lakewalk.

Taking its name from a rescue mutt named Bear who was designated the shop mascot, Hucklebeary started as a pop-up shop that proved so successful, owner Emily Ekstrom decided to invest in buying a permanent storefront space that she's since turned into a bright and inviting space to shop for celebration supplies: cards, gifts, and decorations.

Speaking of decorations, Hucklebeary shares space with Laural Schultze, a local legend under her business name Lauralloons. Schultze can and will make just about anything out of balloons—including, once, a scale model of the St. Louis County Depot—and chances are you'll spot an example of her work in the Hucklebeary display windows.

218 E Superior St., 218-464-0524
hucklebearyduluth.com

FEAST YOUR EYES
AT AN ART GALLERY

With its unparalleled natural beauty and its location in a state nationally known for supporting the arts, Duluth, of course, has a wealth of art to enjoy. In addition to the nonprofit Duluth Art Institute and the university-based Tweed Museum of Art, the city is home to several art galleries that welcome visitors interested in window-shopping. If that becomes actual shopping, all the better.

Joseph Nease Gallery and Prøve Gallery, downtown, host ambitious shows by artists pushing the boundaries of form and content. Canal Park is home to a handful of galleries that are generally oriented more toward retail sales, so if you're looking for a piece of Duluth to hang on your wall, you might start there. That's just the tip of the iceberg, though: the city is also home to superb textile artists like renowned quilter Karen McTavish. You're apt to find art everywhere you look.

Joseph Nease Gallery
23 W 1st St., 218-481-7750
josephneasegallery.com

Prøve Gallery
21 N Lake Ave., 218-428-3001
provecollective.org

GET THRIFTY
AT LOCAL REUSE SHOPS

If you're the kind of person who likes to go thrifting, Duluth has plenty of fertile ground to explore. The city's shops for used clothing and other goods aren't centralized, though, so you'll want to form a plan of attack.

If you're looking for fresh recycled threads, Dannie Duluth and Ragstock are well stocked with a range of options from practical to quirky to kitschy. Reused athletic wear is a world unto itself, with the Duluth Gear Exchange and Play It Again Sports offering opportunities to pick up equipment suited for the local climate without draining your savings.

Father Time Antiques, in Canal Park, is an adventure into the past with plenty of local color represented among the vintage artifacts on sale. Vinyl enthusiasts will want to visit Duluth's only store centered on recorded music: River City Records & Books in Lincoln Park.

THRIFTING OPTIONS

Dannie Duluth

932 E 4th St., 218-724-8507
dannieduluth.com

Ragstock

9 W Superior St., 218-722-1201
ragstock.com

Duluth Gear Exchange

510 E 4th St., 218-481-7270
duluthgearexchange.com

Play It Again Sports

1256 W Arrowhead Rd., 218-724-1700
playitagainsports.com/locations/duluth-mn

Father Time Antiques

395 S Lake Ave., 218-625-2379

River City Records & Books

1814 W Superior St., 218-464-1045
rivercityduluth.com

MAKE YOUR OWN
LAKE SUPERIOR ART GLASS

It's hard to miss the crowds often gathered around the large, open entry to a store on Canal Park Drive. That's Lake Superior Art Glass, where glassmaking demonstrations attract gawkers who marvel at the wonders worked by the shop's experienced craftspeople.

You can, and should, do more than just watch. Seasonally changing classes allow aspiring glass artists to design custom products ranging from bird feeders to candles to decorative flowers. Collaborations with neighboring businesses mean that you might make a one-of-a-kind pint glass to be filled with beer at Hoops Brewing or an ice cream dish to hold a frozen treat from Love Creamery.

If you graduate from beginner classes, you can take advantage of opportunities to learn further techniques. Whether or not you try your own hand, it's worth a visit to see the display of glasswork by nationally known artists.

357 Canal Park Dr., 218-464-1799
lakesuperiorartglass.com

ACTIVITIES BY SEASON

WINTER

SPRING

SUMMER

FALL

SUGGESTED ITINERARIES

DATE NIGHT

KIDS' DAY OUT

ON THE WATER

MOVE YOUR BODY

QUIRKY CHECKLIST

MUSEUM MAVEN

FOOD AND DRINK CRAWL

SPECTACULAR SCENERY

INDEX